# The Digital Millennium Copyright Act

# The Digital Millennium Copyright Act

*Marcia Wilbur*

Writers Club Press
San Jose  New York  Lincoln  Shanghai

# The Digital Millennium Copyright Act

Writers Club Press
an imprint of iUniverse.com, Inc.

For information address:
iUniverse.com, Inc.
5220 S 16th, Ste. 200
Lincoln, NE 68512
www.iuniverse.com

ISBN: 0-595-16004-2

Printed in the United States of America

This book is just to let people know there is a DMCA. Currently, I am working with Rares Marian on another book which includes more legal implications of the Act.

For Updates go to: http://www.dmcasucks.org

At the end of the book is DMCA text. This appendix can be used as a reference to the remainder of the book.

The copiled comments were given to the author with permission granted to publish.

# Contents

# Introduction
## Is hyperlinking illegal?

According to several recent verdicts in lower courts, *Yes.*

That is right, watch out if you want to link your site to another with illegal software. The judges verdicts are in.

In the case of CP4Break, the software was deemed to be illegal. Hyperlinking to the software or a site that contained the software, CPHACK, was also considered to be an illegal act.

Despite this verdict, Time Digital has an active hyperlink to a site that has cphack.

*http://www.time.com/time/digital/daily/0,2822,42129,00.html*

In an ironic twist of fate, Time Warner was involved in a lawsuit as a plantiff with the Motion Picture Association of America against people posting DeCSS. Time, who links to illegal software, was now in court regarding DeCSS. DeCSS was considered by MPAA to be illegal software used to circumvent encryption and violate the DMCA.

## The verdict:

DeCSS is illegal software and hyperlinking to DeCSS (product/service/device) or mirror sites, is also illegal.

## What about free speech?

In Junger v. Daley, the Court ruled that CODE IS SPEECH. At least, code is speech until it's compiled.

## Hyperlinking is a crime?

## As a webmaster, I need to wonder, what does this mean to me?

*Can I upload the files my clients request?*
*Who is ultimately responsible, legally, for my work?*
*Will I be found at fault for uploading something?*
*Will I be found guilty for creating a hyperlink my client or supervisor requests?*

There are no clear laws to answer my statements, at least none that I am aware of.

In April, I met with Connecticut Congressman Sam Gejdenson. *http://www.house.gov/gejdenson/*

He did not respond to these questions. I received a follow up letter from him informing me there about future plans to protect databases. However, there was nothing relevant in that letter to my inquiries about hyperlinking and the DMCA.

*Here are some more questions:*

## If a disgruntled employee decides to add a questionable link or software, who is responsible?

## How can you prove the employee committed this act ?

By the way, what is the penalty for creating a hyperlink anyways?

*Can the judge shut down your site?*
*Can the judge force your host to discontinue to host you?*
(Can't you just get another host?.)

**What are the penalties for creating a hyperlink?**

*Can they take away your computer?*

In a recent case in Oklahoma, a student's computer was seized because he was allegedly infringing on copyrights. The police obtained a search warrant and seized the young man's computer. In the future, could the police seize your computer for creating a hyperlink?

**What is the penalty for linking to illegal software?**

**Have you ever used a search engine to find illegal software?**

**How many links return?**

Sometimes in the thousands.

**Will search engines be penalized too?**

**Then will there be regulations as to who can be a search engine?**

These are just some of the questions that led me to write this book. I hope that you will ponder some of these questions too. These are things that can affect our future.

# Chapter 1

# *Copyright History*

## Copyright Office History

**May 31, 1790**—First federal copyright law enacted.

Claims are to be recorded by clerks of the U.S. District courts.

**1790**—First work registered: The Philadelphia Spelling Book by John Barry.

In 1790, the first copyright law protected:

Books

Maps

Charts

**19th century**—ADDED

1831—Music

1856—Dramatic compositions

1865—Photographs

1870—Works of art

1897—Music (protection against unauthorized public performance)

**1870**—Copyright functions centralized in the Library of Congress. Ainsworth Rand Spofford, Librarian of Congress.

**1897**—Copyright Office becomes a separate department of the Library of Congress Thorvald Solberg, first Register of Copyrights.

**20th century—ADDED**

1909—Certain classes of unpublished works

1912—Motion pictures (previously registered as photographs)

1953—Recording and performing rights extended to nondramatic literary works

1972—Sound recordings fixed and first published on or after Feb. 15

1980—Copyright law amended regarding computer programs

1984—Protection for mask works under the Semiconductor Chip Protection Act

1990—Architectural works were added. Also, additional rights granted to owners of copyright in computer programs regarding rental, lease or lending for commercial purposes, whether direct or indirect.

**1947**—Copyright law put into Title 17, United States Code

**1994**—Copyright Office has recorded 25,733, 511 registrations

**Has U.S. copyright law always provided the same length of term?**

No.

1790—Fourteen years—with a renewal term of 14 more

1831—Twenty-eight years—with a renewal term of 14 more

1909—Publication date, otherwise 28 years with a renewal term of 28 more

1976—New Copyright Act, effective January 1, 1978

Term of protection is the life of the author plus 50 years, measured from when work is first fixed in tangible form.

If the work is of corporate authorship, then coverage is for 75 years from publication, or 100 years from creation, which ever is first

For works with copyright prior to, but still under protection as of 1/1/78, renewal was extended from 28 to 47 years.

Total protection : 75 years

For works with copyright prior to 1/1/78, but expired (I.e. in the public domain) as of that date, total protection possible was 56 years.

1992—Renewal registration optional.

Works for which copyright was secured between January 1, 1964 and December 31, 1977 are automatically renewed, even when not registered.

1998—Sonny Bono Copyright Term Extension Act extended the copyright term for still protected works by 20 years.

**Copyright term under the Sonny Bono Copyright Term**

**Extension is :**

Life of the author (or last surviving author for works of joint authorship) + 70

For works of corporate or unknown authorship, term is the shorter of 95 years from publication, or 120 years from creation.

Copyright for monetary gain has only been in effect for the last few decades. The original basis for copyright was to free people for advancement in the arts and sciences.

Some of the pending/new laws in the copyright section of www.loc.gov

H.R. 89     Satellite Access to Local Stations Act

                                                    1/6/99

H.R. 354    Collections of Information Antipiracy Act

                                                    1/19/99

S. 95       Trading Information Act

                                                    1/19/99

S. 247      Satellite Home Viewers Improvements Act

                                                    1/19/99

S. 303      Satellite Television Act

                                                    1/25/99

H.R. 768    Copyright Compulsory License Improvement Act

2/23/99

H.R. 851    Save Our Satellites Act of 1999

2/25/99

H.R. 1027   Satellite Television Improvement Act

3/8/99

H.R. 1189 Technical Corrections

3/18/99

H.R. 1554   Satellite Copyright, Competition, and Consumer Protection Act of 1999

4/26/99

H.R. 1761   Copyright Damages Improvement Act

5/11/99

H.R. 1858   Consumer and Investor Access to Information Act

5/19/99

S. 1257    Digital Theft Deterrence and Copyright Damages Improvement Act

6/22/99

S. 1260    P.L. 106-44    Technical Corrections in Title 17

6/22/99

S. 1835    Intellectual Property Protection Restoration Act

10/29/99

S. 1948    P.L. 106-113

Intellectual Property and Communications Omnibus Reform Act of 1999

11/17/99

H.R. 3456 P.L. 106-160

Digital Theft Deterrence and Copyright Damages Improvement Act of 1999 11/18/99

# Chapter 2

# History of DMCA

**What started the DMCA ball rolling?**

This information can be found in more full detail at

http://www.loc.gov in the copyright section.

Well, it all started with the WIPO or the World Intellectual Property Organization. The WIPO, Dec 1996, in Geneva, Switzerland adopted a new treaty regarding copyright issues. This treaty included digital issues. The treaty supposedly was NOT to impose unreasonable restrictions on consumer home recording.

**What is the WIPO?**

World Intellectual Property Organization.

**What happened after that?**

Patent and Trademark Office, **May 1997**, began a proposal that went far past the WIPO treaty. One proposal was to restrict lawful fair use copying. The frightening part of this proposal was that it was supposedly to deny the public any new models of VCRs and computers unless we, the consumer, conform to all anti-copy technologies. This was to be imposed upon us, the consumer without regard for expense, malfuntion, inconvience or consumer fair use.

## June 1998

House Commerce Telecommunications Subcommittee holds hearings on HR 2281(DMCA).

Two weeks later the subcommittee changes it for improvement and gives it to the Commerce Committee.

## July 1998

Full House Commerce Committee endorses the changes of its Telecommunications Subcommittee to HR 2281, adds an important "fair use" amendment, and passes it out of committee.

## Aug 1998

HR 2281 passes the House of Representatives.

## Sept 1998

House/Senate Conference Committee begins deliberations on HR 2281. Intense negotiations ultimately produce final bill with benefits to consumers, consumer electronics retailers and professional servicers, libraries and library users, and schools.

## Oct 1998

DMCA receives final approval by the Senate and House of Representatives and is signed into law by President Clinton. (see Appendix III and Appendix V)

## May 1999

HRRC submits statement in support of the use of DTV to a Federal Communication Commission Office of Engineering and Technology's roundtable on DTV receiver compatibility with cable television service.

## Oct 1999

HRRC testifies before House Commerce Telecommunications Subcommittee oversight hearing on situation one year after passage of Digital Millennium Copyright Act and cautions against changes in home recording rules agreed to under the Act.

## March 2000

First DMCA protest held in Washington D.C.

## OCTOBER 28, 2000

**2 years from date of enactment**

# Chapter 3

# *What is it?*
# *What does it mean to you?*

The DMCA was enacted in October of 1998. Some of it's parts are not enforced until two years from the date of enactment.

Full text of the law can be found at

<http://www.eff.org/ip/DMCA/hr2281_dmca_law_19981020_pl1 05-304.html>

The digital millenium copyright act was put into law Oct. 1998. This law is being used to harass people who have placed free software that is being used to watch DVDs on Linux boxes.

**This law could adversely affect anyone, even YOU.**

The DMCA gives large corporations extensive power over the consumer. In a comment made on slashdot.org, streetlawyer summed it up like this:

"Nobody knows what model we should have for promoting creative works.

But nobody will be able to develop that model if we pass an act early on in the process, which will stunt development and create a powerful interest group.

The DMCA is an act of violence by the vested interest, attempting to seize by force something which we currently regard as common property.

We're in a situation analagous to the American Indians when they met up with people who (unlike them) had the concept of private property. We should thank our lucky stars that the property-in-speech lobby can grab our property without also massacring us."

There is currently a case in Connecticut (http://cryptome.org/dvd-mpaa-v-4.htm#Connecticut) <http://cryp-tome.org/dvd-mpaa-v-4.htm>

One major point the suit is trying to make is saying the young man is providing software that violates Sec. 1201. Circumvention of copyright protection systems

(a) VIOLATIONS REGARDING CIRCUMVENTION OF TECHNOLOGICAL MEASURES- (1)(A) No person shall circumvent a technological measure that effectively controls access to a work protected under this title. The prohibition contained in the preceding sentence shall take effect at the end of the 2-year period beginning on the date of the enactment of this chapter.

This young man is being sued by members of the MPAA, such as Time/Warner and Disney. They are using the DMCA as a grounds for the lawsuit. This person simply uploaded a file to a server which is not his own and uploaded a page with a link to the server on to the server.

**What is the definition of providing/offering?**

They say he "offered/provided it." If I created a link to the same server, would I be considered as "offering it"?

**What if someone else had created that site? Would the creator of the site be liable? Even if the domain owner requested such a link?**

And, What if by some unforseen reason, someone was able to get access(hack) to MPAA server and upload the file and place a link on their main page, would MPAA be in violation of 1201?

I understand there may be third party liability restrictions for people who create a link to a page which holds the link to the server which contains the file.

**But someday (speculating), could you be liable for a "HYPER-LINK"???**

**Has that day come?**

We can argue the point that Hughes no more provided the file any more than Google or any search engine or other site with the file link did.

However, one response is, that he offered the file the same way the local newspaper gives away free newspapers at the convenience store.

**What is the difference between a digital file and paper?**

But there is one big difference.

The paper, um, that's tangible! The owner of the store knows it is there... The data file is not tangible and the owner of the server did not know it was there, probably.

It is reasonable to agree there needs to be two sets of laws, one for the tangible world and one for the intangible.

At a Berkman Center for Internet and Society conference the idea was presented that the legal community does not want computer science community involved in legislature due to the fact that there might be a conflict of interest.

## What about precendence?

These court proceedings could set a precedence.

At this point the proceedings are civil.

But I ask you,

## what if... what if... they could go to criminal next time?

There will be precendence due to these current cases.

Although many may argue that the file is in bad taste, DeCSS does promote use on a Linux system. Irregardless of other Linux system decoders on the market, available or not, you should be able to choose how you want to watch a DVD. After you purchase the DVD, you should be able to enjoy at your leisure. You could use it as a frisbee or make a clock out of it. You should be able to create your own DVD player if you wish! And so, you should be able to crack their unfunctional code and use it on another machine. But, according to the DMCA, this is NOT permitted.

## Is this a "free country" we live in?

According to the text of the DMCA, it would be illegal for Stephen King to view his ebook online. According to the article *<http://www.lawnewsnetwork.com/practice/techlaw/news/A20129-*

*2000Mar30.html>* King uses a macintosh and the format for the ebook is downloadable to a PC.

There has also been speculation in the computer science community of not being able to use other things that are cross-platform using this DMCA.

*One example given was that you may be restricted to only use MS Word to Open MS Word Documents.*

## Can this be true?

For all of those people who have Star Office or another word processing software package that they use at home, **what does this mean to you?**

## Is this thing getting out of hand?

Here are some potential problems that may have or may occur when dealing with Internet or CyberLaw. This list was developed partially by the author from an outline developed by the members of Openlaw.

The court doesn't have jurisdiction (wrong parties, procedural problems).

Plaintiffs aren't real parties in interest.

Cannot prove defendents committed actual offense (uploading, etc.)

It could be argued that software doesn't circumvent. It permits use, not access—no 1201(a)(2) violation

In the case of movies, the movie owner already has authority to access

The software doesn't give access, the PLAYER does.

If software circumvents, it's within one of the exceptions

*Reverse engineering*

*Encryption research*

*Software may not be a "technology, product, service, device, component, or part thereof"*

*Commercially significant purpose or use other than circumvention AND not primarily designed or marketed for circumvention*

## 1201 is unconstitutional

*Puts too much burden on free speech*

*Software is speech*

*Takes away fair use (fair use is constitutionally mandated )*

*Outside congressional power (Copyright or Commerce)*

*Potentially unlimited times*

*Patent-like monopoly without the patent-requisite disclosure*

*Anitrust problems / copyright misuse*

*Unsound*

*Vague*

> *Impermissible delegation to private entities*

# Chapter 4

# Congress shall enact no law—
# 1st ammendment

## CONSTITUTION
## OF THE
## UNTIED STATES

We the People of the United States, in Order to form a more perfect Union, establish Justice, insure domestic Tranquility, provide
for the common defence, promote the general Welfare, and secure
the Blessings of Liberty to ourselves and our Posterity, do ordain
and establish this Constitution for the United States of Amercia.

(ARTICLES I-VII follow)

## AMENDMENTS
## TO THE
## CONSTITUTION
## OF THE
## UNITED STATES
## OF
## AMERICA

## Amendment 1*

**Congress shall make no law** respecting an establishment of religion, or prohibiting the free exercise thereof; or **abridging the freedom of speech**, or of the press, or the right of the people peacably to assemble, and to petition the Government for a redress of grievances.

*The Bill of Rights (first 10 Amendments) were ratified effective December 15, 1791.

## What are some of the limitations under Copyright Law?

Copyright covers the *form* of expression, not the substance of the content.

Rights are not unlimited. Sections 107-121 of the 1976 Copyright Act establish the limitations.

A major limitation to copyright: the Doctrine of 'Fair Use' in Section 107.

## What is the Doctrine of Fair Use?

The Doctrine of Fair Use was not mentioned in earlier copyright laws

Fair Use was developed over a number of years through court cases

It covers purposes for which reproduction may be considered 'FAIR'and there are a few factors used to determine the fairness of a particular use

## What are the factors used to determine fairness?

*What is the nature of the copyrighted work?*

*What is the purpose and character of the use?*

*Is it commercial?*

*Is it for nonprofit educational use?*

*How much of the work is used in comparision to the whole?*

*What effect does the use have on the potential market for or value of the copyrighted work?*

## What are some purposes for which fair use may be used?

Criticism

Comment

Parody

Research

News media

Scholarship

Teaching

## What types of works are protected by copyright?

Literary works

Musical works, with the words

Dramatic works, with the music

Pantomimes and choreographic works

Pictorial, graphic and sculptural works

Motion pictures and audiovisual works

Sound recordings

Architectural works

**What about works not specifically listed?**

The court looks at the categories in a broad way.

There is a review Copyright Office documents for information.

For example:

Computer programs may be registered as 'literary works'

Computer programs are not a "work in progress".

Maps may be registered as 'pictorial works'.

**What is NOT protected by copyright?**

Works not fixed in a tangible form of expression

Titles, names, slogans, short phrases, familiar designs or symbols, variations of typographic ornamentation, lettering, or coloring, listings of contents or ingredients

Ideas, ^^^^^**procedures**^^^^^, methods, systems, processes, concepts, principles, discoveries, or devices, as distinguished from a description, explanation, or illustration.

Works consisting completely of public property information and containing no original writing.

***What is a procedure? Isn't encryption considered a procedure to secure? ****

Has U.S. copyright laws always protected all of these works?

No!

# Chapter 5

# Code is Speech
## Encryption therefore is speech?

**CRYPTOGRAPHY:**

Cryptography is the science of secret writing, a science that

has roots stretching back hundreds, and perhaps thousands, of

years. The idea is to encrypt works to only be read by intended parties.

**ENCRYPTION:**

Encryption is the **process** of converting a message from its original

form ("plaintext") into a scrambled form ("ciphertext").

Encryption usually utilizes an algorithm and a key that acts as a password.

**DECRYPTION:**

Decryption is the translation back to plaintext when

the message is received by someone with a "key."

**What is not protected by copyright?**
Works not fixed in a tangible form of expression

Ideas, ^^^^^**procedures**^^^^^, methods, systems, processes, concepts, principles,

discoveries, or devices, as distinguished from a description,

explanation, or illustration.

***What is a procedure? Isn't encryption considered a procedure to secure? ****

### junger v. daley

Peter D. Junger tried to post some encryption code on his class web site and thus ended up in federal court. His arguemnt was that code is speech and should have full First Amendment protection as free speech.

The government argued that source code is a not a form of speech, but functional as a device.

Junger's Website

*http://samsara.law.cwru.edu/~sftspch/*

Judge Gwin of the United States District Court for the Northern District of Ohio ruled encryption source code is not expressive and is not protected by the First Amendment.

The Sixth Circuit Court of Appeals found that "computer source code is an express means for the exchange of information and ideas about computer programming"

Professor Junger is a law professor at Case Western Reserve University in Cleveland (not to be confused with the case _Junger_ )

## BERNSTEIN CASE

Snuffle and Unsnuffle.

Encryption code is speech. Daniel Bernstein, a mathematician, challenged the export control laws on encryption on First Amendment grounds. Professor Bernstein claimed that his right to publish his own encryption software and share his research results with others over the Internet was being unconstitutionally restricted by the government's export controls.

The government argued that the computer source code for programs are not protected by the First Amendment because it is a tool used to encrypt messages rather than a language used to express them.

The case won an appeal in the Ninth Circuit Court of Appeals. Federal District Court Judge Patel ruled computer programs as speech and are thereby protected by the First Amendment.

"This court can find no meaningful difference between computer language…and German or French,"

## *Chapter 6*

# *Movies*

## OLD VCRS/NEW PROTECTION TECHNIQUES

Old vcrs can tape new movies that have been striped in order to protect them from being copied. Is this using a device to bypass encryption?

**Would using an old vcr to tape a movie be considered circumventing?**

**What about the Dual vcr? What of that?**

These are interesting questions. Owning an older VCR/Camcorder is a violation of the DMCA.

**Does this mean you cannot develop a DVD player?**

In order to test it, I will need to break the encryption of the DVD.

**Is it against the law to create a device that will play DVDs that I own?**

Can that be true?
In the case of DeCSS, yes it is true.

> You cannot create software to watch a dvd you have already purchased to watch because you can not circumvent the encryption. That is a violation of the DMCA.

What this means is that we are not allowed to crack codes. That is what I get from it.

**What happens to this country if it is illegal to break encryption? What secrets can be hidden if we are not even p ermitted to break encryption?**

Here are some intersting thoughts to ponder:

**How much does a DVD player cost?**

**Who makes the DVDs?**
**Who makes the DVD players?**

**DECSS**

**DeCSS—Restricting Internet Freedoms such as Hyperlinking**

Question 1:

*Why would the Motion Picture Association of America (Disney, Time Warner, Paramount, Universal Studios, MGM, Tristar, Columbia, 20th Century Fox) bring about a lawsuit and attempt to stop hyperlinking to software that is not illegal?*

In the last few years the Internet and WWW population and use has boomed to extraordinary levels. The face of entertainment is changing. Rather than watch movies, many people are surfing, shopping online, chatting, reading ebooks, playing video games, learning about their favorite topic online, etc. Media giants such as Time Warner are bound to lose some money. Big media companies, in the past, have controlled what we watch on television, our news, our entertainment, our movies, even cartoons. They literally report on what they want to report.

If you search Time and Time Digital for any information on this lawsuit MPAA vs. DeCSS, you may find one short article.

**Why wasn't there much mention of the DeCSS lawsuit with the MPAA until late?**

Maybe Time Warner doesn't want people to know about DeCSS. The lawsuit is intended to keep people from posting or even linking to DeCSS. MPAA president Jack Valenti gave a deposition and the plaintiff's lawyers wanted to keep that deposition from the media. *<http://cryptome.org/mpaa-v-2600-jvd.htm>*

**Would you be interested in hearing Michael Eisner of Disney's deposition?**

I would, but apparently, according to web rumor, the plaintiffs in the case told the judge that Mr. Eisner will not be giving his deposition.

The court was a bit confused, as that is up to the court and not the lawyers of the plaintiff. DeCSS was never found to be illegal, however an injunction was filed against the 2600 site(s) restricting them from *linking to links* that contained the DeCSS software!

**From the *<http://ct2600.org/dvd-info>* site** : On 01.21.00 the CA (then the NY) courts allowed an injunction against posting the DeCSS/AUTH code.

ct2600.org will no loger be able to mirror or post these files/code in any way. (I believe he meant, they will no LONGER be able to mirror the files/code in any way)

## Question 2:

### What law would enable them to do so?

The ever popular Digital Millenium Copyright Act—DMCA

### What is DeCSS?

DeCSS is a software program developed to enable users of the Linux operating system to view DVDs on their computers. Until recently, DVDs could not be viewed using the Linux operating system. In order to develop this software package, the encryption of CSS code for DVD encryption was broken. The Motion Picture Association of America, which includes such names as Time Warner, Disney, Paramount, MGM, TriStar, Universal, Columbia, et al sued to keep DeCSS from being posted or linked. The inability to link or post DeCSS would reduce the amount of people able to *use* DeCSS.

### What is the CSS scramble?

CSS is the encryption code. It was first posted anonymously on LiVid on October 25, 1999. Although Jon Johansen has been rumored and interviewed as having written DeCSS, and although he is currently a "master of reverse engineering", it is rumored that he was NOT a master of reverse engineering at the time of the CSS crack. As a matter of fact, it is rumored that the Masters didn't even exist at the time of the CSS cracking.

### Where can DeCSS be found?

DeCSS is all over the Internet. It can be found by doing a search online. A user can find many links to the code and software using any search engine online.

**What is the cost to copy a DVD?**

That is the strange part. It would likely cost MORE to copy one DVD than to buy one in the store. As far as online access, those would be giant files.

It's cheaper and easier to rent or buy!

**Why have these sites been targets of lawsuits while search engines and other sites remain blameless?**

**Time Digital actively links to mirrors of illegal software? So why can't 2600 link to DeCSS? In this article, Time actively links to 3 CPHack mirror sites.**

The last of the three sites it links to has a direct download to Illegal Software!

*http://www.time.com/time/digital/daily/0,2822,42129,00.html*

**Due Process:**

By placing an injunction, wouldn't that be a violation of Due Process?

… life, liberty, and property…even intellectual property. Patented works fall under the property category, why not DeCSS?

**Who owns software?**

You could read an entire book on this matter. Who owns the software? If software is not patent issued software—who is the rightful property owner? If software is freeware or shareware, isn't that software considered to be the property of the person who downloaded it? Isn't it property of who is using it or has it lawfully residing on their server for others to download or use? Do you own shareware or freeware?

What if someone filed an injunction against you and told you that you can not have that software on your website.

No, the software was *not* found to be illegal or damaging to anyone. However, a media giant such as the Motion Picture Association with all of its legal department, has decided they do not like the software on your site. Maybe they don't like the software because it allows users to use technology without buying an expensive playing device. In any case, you are forced by the court, without any due process, to remove the software from your site. That is a violation of your constitutional rights. The fourteenth amendment prohibits a State from depriving a person of property without due process of law. But wait, there's more!

**Not able to decrypt?**

According to the DMCA—Digital Millenium Copyright Act, we are not able to decrypt any technology or technology device etc…that is related to copyright materials. This, is a violation of our constitutional rights as well. The first amendment of the Constitution of the United States of America: "**Congress shall make no law** respecting an establishment of religion, or prohibiting the free exercise thereof; or **abridging the freedom of speech**, or of the press; or the right of the people peaceably to assemble, and to petition the government for a redress of grievances. " (emphasis added)

When you get a chance please go to this link and read about freedom of speech and interference by the government.
*<http://wwwsecure.law.cornell.edu/topics/first_amendment.html>*

If the government is interfering with the right of free speech in order to regulate the content of the speech, the Supreme Court requires justification for that.

**Code is speech. Is encryption speech?**

In the Junger v. Daley decision, code is speech, in it's uncompiled format. So, wouldn't encryption be considered speech in the same vein? Isn't pig latin speech?

**Why would an Internet Service Provider like AOL buy Time Warner, when Time Warner is currently involved in a lawsuit which has sought to restrict Internet freedoms, such as hyperlinking?**

With all the lawsuits filed against AOL lately I began to wonder, why would they buy Time Warner?

**What is happening over at America Online?**

AOL has been involved in several class actions suits in the past. In June, I spoke with *Nicholas Graham* of the media department at America Onlne. He assured me that AOL is probably aware of the lawsuit involving Time Warner and the Motion Picture Association of America against defendants linking to DeCSS. Mr Graham also informed me that the merger with Time Warner will not be completed until Fall 2000 because of regulatory paperwork and process. I did ask him if there was any posted statement on the matter and he informed me that there is not now, because the merger is not finalized. He did inform me that it was possible a statement would be made once the merger is complete around the fall of this year.

**What if Hyperlinking becomes illegal? Is it already? Can those judgements stick?**

The hyperlinking police?!
For anyone who owns a site or is a web developer, this issue is very disturbing.

**Who will be found liable for something that is sent to a server?**

**Is the owner of the website responsible for software that is found on the server?**

**Is the ISP responsible, or is the responsibility on the web developer?**

According to the DMCA, there is exemption for ISPs but not for developers.

**What if someone at the company in question told a web dev person to upload DeCSS?**
**Is the web dev person responsible?**

**And what if, heaven forbid, some developer decides out of spite or any reason to upload "questionable" materials to the server?**

**Is the owner of the site responsible for that?**
**What is the owner of the site's legal responsibilities?**

A future in Computer law or Cyberlaw will be challenging.
To find more about DeCSS
> *<http://eon.law.harvard.edu/openlaw/DVD/resources.html>*
> *<http://www.wired.com/news/politics/0,1283,35394,00.html>*

# Chapter 7

# Conference Notes
# *Signal or Noise: The future of music on the net*
# *A Berkman Center for Internet and Society Event*

**Intellectual Property in Cyberspace—Online Lecture and Discussion Series**

Friday, February 25, 2000 I rented a Ford Ranger and drove the 130 or so miles to Cambridge first thing in the morning. I showed up at the conference at Harvard Law School's Austin Hall. This conference, Signal or Noise, was sponsored by the Berkman Center for Internet and Society and the EFF: Electronic Frontier Foundation. YES. I knew this was going to be an awesome conference.

The place was full of freaks, geeks and lawyers. But seriously, it was a diverse crowd. They were late starting, it was a small group of about 75 in attendance. Charles Nesson was the first to speak. He acknowledged Glenn Brown's work in coordinating the function. Glenn, a shy, handsome, young man, humbly spoke a few intelligent words of welcome. It was a humorous gathering. The tone was light hearted and fun.

The panel included:
Peter Harter representing Emusic(<*http://www.emusic.com)*> Jeff

Rayport from Harvard's business school Richard Reimer, Vice President of Legal Affairs, ASCAP (also known as the "evil empire") Brian Zisk of Green Witch Radio (*<http://www.greenwitch.com)>* Steve Fabrizio—was on the agenda but did not attend. RIAA (*<http://www.riaa.org)>*

The topics were interesting. Basically what I learned was that for years, the artists and songwriters in the music industry have not been adequately compensated in relation to monies earned by sales. The artists receive a very small percentage of the take on CDs. This is one reason CDs are not sold at concerts, because a large percentage of the money doesn't go directly to the band.

They discussed SDMI(*<http://www.sdmi.org).>* SDMI is an organization trying to make standards or specifications but clearly have a conflict of interest. Mr. John Gilmore (*<http://www.toad.com/gnu),>* a former programmer, now civil libertarian, referred to it as the "fox guarding the henhouse".

I also began to realize that it would be difficult to truly compensate artists with all the Napster(http://www.napster.com*)/MP3s(http://www.mp3.com)* floating around online.

At lunch I overheard the Richard Reimer from ASCAP discussing AOL/Time Warner and I realized that a majority of this crowd might have a great understanding of the law but little computer knowledge. (I also realized that they had put his name on his name tag incorrectly as Robert.)

Panel 2
10:45—12:00 Intellectual Property, Will Technology Kill It, or only make it stronger?

People on the panel.

Eric Scheirer: MIT Media Lab
Eric Hellweg: Senior Editor Business 2.0
Terry Fisher: Professor, Harvard Law School
Frank Davis: Internet Director, Astralwerks.
Karlheim Brandenburg: Fraunhofer IIS Studio Department

This panel consisted of a more interesting and contentious group. I was truly impressed by Karlheim Brandenburg from the Fraunhofer IIS Studio Department. He was brillant and tactfully amusing. The moderator, Jonathan Zittrain, showed us a site... *<http://www.trust-edpc.com.>* I began to heartily laugh at this site. Please visit this site if you haven't already. It is a consortium of Microsoft, IBM and some others who are trying to instill a greater trust of their product globally. No surprise there. However, the moderator asked anyone in the audience to explain what this page meant. I really thought he was being sarcastic. However, Mr. Brandenburg tactfully and pleasantly explained that there are computer companies that are more trusted in the computing world. It was quite amusing. I quite often amused by Microsoft. In an ironical turn of events, when I got home and tried to load that page, my computer crashed... I am running Windows 95. The professor, Terry Fisher, inadvertently opened the debugger at the Napster site and then closed IE. Which just shows that we need more people with computer knowledge working with the lawmakers. However, I got an impression that some lawmakers don't want computer people involved in lawmaking. In other words, they believe that computer scientists are the ones causing these problems and this would be a conflict of interest.

I had thought during this time that technology that protects music from being played/recorded would be a good way to go. Mr. Scheirer discussed the work on MP4. Personally, I don't think that MP4 is going to go anywhere. However, I could be wrong. It won't come out for another 3-5 years so who knows, anything can happen between now and then. They discussed better compression, Virtual Reality, games, interactive music, etc. There was discussion on taxing computers to pay for creative costs. The people representing, or working with the record industry, believe that they are in power, they have control of it all. They believe that they can put the music on another platform and people will buy it. A secure format might be used. I bought into this theory UNTIL I heard Chuck D.

Mistachuck, Public Enemy musician. A visionary man. He asked the audience who believed that CDs as we know it will be a thing of the past in two years. I raised my hand. And I admit, I felt extremely stupid because I was the only one with my hand held high. I felt stupid until, Chuck began to speak. And then, it all came together for me. You see, I believe that we, the public, have been conned. We have been told, or shown the music we can listen to. You see, there is so much more music out there. Have you ever heard Japanese Reggae? The record companies, only allow the music they chose to be available to the public. So you see, the internet allows more music to be available. The music industry could collapse, but it could be like when the personal video camera came out. The movie industry did not collapse. However, we got to see a lot of funny home videos. But music, could be different. If I can listen to something free online that is downloadable, then why am I going to pay 18 dollars for a cd??? Music companies online will be able to compete with big music and this music online will bring hope to struggling musicians. I liked Chuck D. I would venture to say his ideas are progressive. With effort and success he and others will be able to compete with Sony or BMG or whomever else. I think it is amazing what rapstation is doing and personally, I applaud him. His url is *<http://www.rapstation.com.>* He has 5 studios for recording if anyone is interested.

1:00—2:15 Cybermusicology

Christopher Lydon moderated
Nyssim Lefford
Todd Winkler
Siva Vaidhyanathan
Mark Hossler did not show up
Rob Jaczko

This group was mostly educators and people discussing the future of music and creativity. There were some presentations that followed. One by Willie Henshaw at Rocket Network.

Musicians Empowered online panel started late...

Alex Fowler, EFF—*<http://www.eff.org>*
John Flansburgh, Musician
Ken Wirt, Riffage.com
Scott Llewellyn, Musician/Clerk
Willie Henshaw
Chuck D.

I spoke with the Glenn Brown as I left the building. I was grateful, for the conference had given me much to ponder. I found out from him, that there were exactly ZERO computer science grads pursuing law and are involved at the Berkman Center for Internet and Society. And although I would like to be NUMBER 1 there, I fear that my degree is too far off from being number 1. However, I would encourage anyone going into computer science to consider going to law school thereafter at Harvard or Yale or any state university. And, I will see you in the courtrooms or at the conferences soon.

If computer laws are soley created by lawmakers without a full in depth understanding of the technology, the law will be useless. And if a computer law is created by a computer scientist without any understanding of law, then that law will be useless. Working together, the computer science community and the lawmakers will be able to make laws that will withstand time.

INFO, Link to webcast
*<http://cyber.law.harvard.edu/EVENTS/NETMUSIC.HTML>*
*<http://www.eff.org>* (I joined after the conference!)
*<http://www.rapstation.com>*—chuck d's site
*<http://www.greenwitch.com>*—radio station
*<http://www.emusic.com>*


## More on Napster

Well, as you may or may not have heard, certain members of Metallica are suing Napster.
*<http://www.wired.com/news/politics/0,1283,36154,00.html>*

These cases get more and more complex. I believe that most people would contend that 'stealing' is wrong. However, when is it considered stealing. And frankly, what is considered stealing. It can be related to the abortion issue. Most people would contend that murder is wrong, but when is the fetus considered human?

And so the arguments wage on. Is it stealing to charge $15 dollars for a CD that a consumer only wants to listen to one song? It's unreasonable that consumers haven't had any choice but to buy expensive Cds or albums in the past. Now a lot of consumers are listening to music for free, via Napster, broadcast radio online and other downloadable manners.

When I first realized I could get music downloaded for free online, I was surprised. I questioned the legality of the situation. I only wanted to listen to one Billy Joel song. I found many sites that offered songs for free. (Pre-Napster days) I thought I could just listen to the song and not download it, however it came through as a download as soon as I clicked the link. I didn't know if that was ok or not.

Years later, here we are, hanging on the question... is it ok? And what about wavs of movie phrases. We like to listen to those, don't we. Those funny little wavs like the ones found at

*<http://www.dailywav.com>*

Until the decisions are final, maybe I'll stick to broadcast.com. But what if I record songs from there? What of that?

# Chapter 8

# Other DMCA issues

## Who wrote CPHack? What is CPHack?

Matthew Skala and Eddy Jansson wrote the cp4break package which includes CPHack. This program allows users to view what sites are being blocked by CyberPatrol. CyberPatrol is censorware.

## What is censorware?

Censorware blocks users from viewing certain sites online. These sites that are chosen are mostly unknown. Once CPHack was available, people were able to see which sites were being blocked.

Some of the sites blocked by censorware products are quite surprising. There are certain watchdog groups who are doing experiments with the blocked lists. One of the interesting experiments is copying certain information from mainstream or larger organizations/companies that are prejudice, racist or racy.

The group then posts the site online and gets the company producing the censorware to view it. Once the site is banned by the censorware group, this watchdog organization reveals that the content from that site actually came from a mainstream media company or popular family magazine/site/organization. The logical thing then might be to censor the originating organization. However, I have yet to see this happen.

The results of these types of experiments are quite interesting. Some questions are being raised about certain sites that are banned. There seems to be no reason for such banning.

I know that over a year ago there was a shopping client that would refuse to allow its affiliates to have links or search engines on the page that linked to pornography or questionable sites. Well, I for one, cannot regulate what is in a search engine. Webmasters are certainly not going to remove search engines from sites. Lately though, I have not seen that shopping client around...have you?

## How does the DMCA fit into all of this?

In the case of CPHack, the DMCA was used again. And again the anti circumvention portion of the DMCA was used in order to stop the defendants Skala and Jansson from distributing the software. According to the law, they were in violation of the Digital Millenium Copyright Act.

The anti-circumvention provision of the Digital Millennium Copyright Act "prohibits trafficking in devices whose primary purpose is to circumvent a technology meant to protect copyrighted works".

CPHack certainly qualifies.

## Why?

Because the software, CyberPatrol, is a copyrighted work.

This case was settled. In this case, the defendants sold the software CPHack to the plantiffs. The code for the software was under GNU public license and therefore was free software. The judge, on the other hand, made linking to CPHack illegal. As of today, Time Digital still has active links to CPHack mirrors!

*http://www.time.com/time/digital/daily/0,2822,42129,00.html*

CPHACK
How they did it.
*http://www.usc.edu/~douglast/202/lecture19/cp4break.html*

MATTHEW SKALA's Page
*http://www.islandnet.com/~mskala/*

Eddy L O Jansson's Old Page with a link to his new one
*http://hem.passagen.se/eddy1/index.html*

The BAIT and Switch!
*http://www.peacefire.org/BaitAndSwitch/*

**Other: MPAA is rumored to be suing Scour and Copyleft.**

Conclusion

I recall the words of Jim Savas, an instructor of mine. These words are very true. We were discussing the DMCA and he mentioned that most people would agree that stealing was wrong. As in abortion issues. Most would not deny that killing is wrong. But when is the fetus considered alive. Where is the line? That is wherein the argument is.

My personal opinion is that the DMCA needs improvement. The original basis for copyright was to PROMOTE arts and sciences.

The more voters and taxpayers with voices know and understand the DMCA, the better the chance of improvement.

We must not sit back and watch our liberties restricted because we are too busy making the day to day dollar or because we just don't care.

How will you answer your children, grandchildren, and others when they ask you,

"What happened to hyperlinking?" or "Why didn't anyone try to keep it free?"

or "Why can't I look at that source code?" or "Why can't I reverse engineer?"

I can only begin to speculate at the amount of progress that will be lost due to the restrictions of the DMCA and because of recent copyright law.

For example, in the case of Napster. The technology there is amazing. It can do much more than simply share music files. It has the potential to do a great deal.

And speaking of that case, I must say that to impose on Napster because the users abuse the program would be like imposing on a car manufacturer because people drive drunk.

Would anyone try to sue the phone company because people make crank calls?

A computer is a device that is used to process information.

To me, it's like a giant pencil.

Would you copyright a pencil?

It may have more workings than a pencil, but in reality, the computer is similar to ... a pencil. It is used for nothing but to achieve processes.

The computer processes.

Considering a computer is a processor, then, in fact, you cannot consider encryption to be illegal. Encryption is a procedure. To encrypt is to procede with security. To decrypt is to dissolve the security of the encryption.

These are processes or procedures that are, under copyright law, not considered copyrightable. However, encryption is entered into the DMCA.

Perhaps lobbys and money are more powerful in today's government, than the rules and desires of our founding fathers.

With liberty and justice for all.... AMEN!

# Appendix I
## Protests

**THE PROTEST Tuesday, March 28, 2000**

**PROTEST #1**

The Linux Users Groups et al in the Washington D.C. area held a protest of the DMCA.

When I heard about the protest I considered going. Then I thought it was too far to travel to Washington D.C. from Connecticut. After a little logical thinking, I decided that I really did believe in this protest and I could not face myself in the mirror if I didn't go. So, I got the train to D.C. and arrived in the morning at Union Station at about 6:30 am. It was a quick walk up to the park Capitol.

I didn't know where the park was that was referred to in the instruction sheet, so I asked the police officers at the Capitol. They asked me if there was something going on there. I told them, "oh, I'm just meeting some people there." Incidentally, later in the day while protesting, these two officers told the group to leave the area and take the sidewalk.

When I arrived at the park, it was about 8ish. There was noone there but a couple of joggers. I began to be concerned. Soon after, I saw Serge with the signs and his friend with the banner and I was a little relieved. Apparently, the instructions were to meet at the park, even though Serge had requested to meet elsewhere. He had been up there since 7:15 waiting.

A few other people arrived and soon we seemed to have a pretty good group. We made up the signs, well, that one fellow with the cool us flag jacket made up the signs (no art talent here), and we headed to the area we had a permit to picket. Yes, they even had a permit.

It was a beautiful day. The weather couldn't have been better. We protested around the reflecting pool and took little excursions to the MS trial courthouse.

Some people present were Megan Larko, working under contract at Nasa, Serge W., who works for a Ralph Nader group, Peter Teuben, a hilarious man that cannot view his DVDs he buys from Holland is "annoyed to no end" about it. Timothy Lord from Slashdot showed up along with Declan McCullagh from Wired.

**Eventually we all walked to the Supreme Court and the Library of Congress building. Dave Niemi said a couple of closing words and we went our separate ways.**

Serge was really gung ho about the entire event. He was very persuasive and gave out lots of leaflets. We explained to visiting high school students about DMCA and we got a lot of interest. Everyone was awesome!

I met a lot of interesting people but most of all, we stood up for what we believe in.

**More on the DMCA and protest**

*<http://www.eff.org>*

*<http://slashdot.org/article.pl?sid=00/03/28/1813204&mode=thread>*

*<http://www.astro.umd.edu/~teuben/dmca/>*

*<http://www.wired.com/news/politics/0,1283,35178,00.html>*

*<http://www.linuxworld.com/linuxworld/lw-2000-03/lw-03-dmca.html>*

## Other Protests

**NY LUGS go to D.C.**
*http://lwn.net/2000/0427/a/dmca-protest.html*

**5/5/00 NOVALUGS, NY LUGS and D.C. Lugs**
*http://www.theregister.co.uk/content/archive/10674.html*

**Silicon Valley**
*http://www.svlug.org*

**NY LUGs**
*http://www.nylug.org*

Links pages
Cornell site on Title 17
*http://www4.law.cornell.edu/uscode/17/1201.html*
LOC   *http://www.loc.gov*

# *Appendix II*

DMCA Comments

David Neimi, DC LUGS

Serge Wroclawski, DMCA Protester

Jim Gleason, NY LUGS

Timothy Lord, Writer/Protester

John Young, Cryptome

Emmett Plant, Editor-in-Chief of Linux.com

Don Marti, Technical Editor of Linux Journal

Bryan Taylor, Openlaw

Matthew Skala, CP4Break/CPHack

Wendy Selzer, Openlaw

Gerald Thurman, Educator – computer science

Napster (good link)

# David Neimi
# President Washington D.C. Linux Users Group
# First DMCA Protest Organizer—March 2000

**Currently David is heavily involved in work regarding Virginia UCITA.**

Below is his Protesters guide which can be found at
http://www.tuxlaw.org/dmca/dmca-guide.html

A Protester's Guide to the

Digital Millennium Copyright Act
(U.S. Code Title 17, Chapter 12, Section 1201)

The DMCA was enacted in the fall of 1998, to a great extent justified by new World Intellectual Property Organization (WIPO) treaties which require signatory countries take steps to improve the legal protection afforded to copyrighted materials. Proponents make much of the exceptions and balancing provisions in the DMCA, while failing to note that these vaunted exceptions only apply to some of the provisions, leaving some of the worst provisions unchecked and unbalanced.

Subparagraph (a)(1)(A) forbids circumvention of "a technological measure that effectively controls access to [copyrighted works]." There is no requirement in subparagraph (a)(1)(A) that the access controls be reasonable, appropriate, or even intentional; any arbitrary access control for copyrighted materials of any sort is granted legal reinforcement.

Furthermore, otherwise legitimate and beneficial uses of copyrighted material are made technically difficult or impractical by such access controls are thus legally stymied as well, except as are excepted elsewhere in the DMCA. Note that this subparagraph does not take effect until two years after enactment, which would nominally be in the fall of 2000.

Note also that this subparagraph quite clearly exceeds the Constitutional authority

Congress has to protect copyrights, because the access controls are granted legal protection whether or not they have anything to do with protecting copyrighted material against infringement. It has been speculated that this is a so-called "paracopyright" which would be justified under the commerce clause instead, which, if successful, would throw decades of carefully balanced intellectual property legislation and case law in this country into chaos.

This subparagraph makes a bit more sense if you think of the case of cable TV service, in which the entire business model is vulnerable to theft of service if access controls are violated. But the language used is so broad as to apply to any conceivable service or material containing copyrighted material which contains access controls, whether or not copyright infringement and theft of service are even plausible concerns.

Subparagraphs (a)(1)(B, C, D, and E) establish a review process for determining the exceptions and applicability of (a)(1)(A) above. However, subparagraph (E) explicitly states that the review process cannot ameliorate the effects of other provisions of the DMCA (including the crucial subsections (a)(2) and (b)(1) below).

Subsection (a)(2) prohibits making any utility or device available to the public which is primarily intended to aid circumvention of access controls as discussed in (a)(1) above.

This subsection is much worse than it seems. The exceptions and review process of (a)(1)(B through E) do not apply to this subsection, and even worse, this subsection took effect immediately!

In theory, consumers would still free to personally circumvent access controls in ways which are found to be acceptable by the review process mentioned above. But the outlawing of legal circumvention aids will likely make circumvention of all but the most superficial access controls impractically complex and tedious. This effectively nullifies the effects of the review process and the exceptions in (a)(1), as it will be far easier to prosecute the creators and distributors of circumvention aids than it ever would have been to prosecute individual consumers who engage in circumvention.

There are some indications that Congress thought this paragraph would be used primarily to fight "black boxes" that some people use to gain unauthorized access to cable programming. But the MPAA clearly had other ideas in mind; not surprisingly, this is the paragraph being primarily used by the MPAA in its lawsuits in New York and Connecticut.

Subsection (b)(1) prohibits making any utility or device available to the public which is primarily intended to aid circumvention of technological measures which protect copyright owner rights. The language is similar to Subsection (a)(2), but the access controls here are limited to those which are legitimately within the scope of sanctioned copyright legislation, so this subsection, unlike those in Subsection (a) is probably constitutional.

But this subsection is not without its problems. Even an access control which is designed to protect a legitimate right of a copyright holder may do so in an unnecessarily restrictive way, thereby trampling on the rights and abilities of legitimate users of the copyrighted material. Moreover, a measure (such as DVD Region Coding) which is claimed to reduce copyright infringement may in actuality be relatively useless for its stated purpose and instead be primarily intended to let the copyright holder gain an unfair advantage over its customers.

In order to restrict legal protection to only those access controls which are truly ntended to reduce infringement, a party bringing a case under this subsection should be required to prove all of the following: that the access control is effective at protecting specific rights of copyright holders against infringement; that the infringements against which the access control is effective are ongoing and have a significant detrimental economic effect on the copyright holder; and that the access control keeps restrictions on the fair use and rights of legitimate users to the minimum practical level.

Subsections (c), (d), and (e) provide a number of exceptions and clarifications of subsections (a) and (b). However, none of these exceptions do anything to weaken the ban on circumvention aids. Hence, normal consumers are still just as vulnerable to access controls which eliminate their "fair use" abilities and which prevent them from exercising their rights such as free speech.

Subsection (f) grants an exemption permitting reverse engineering to subsections (a) and (b) above, for the extremely narrow purpose of bypassing access controls in a legally obtained computer program in order to study it in order to create a separate, interoperable program. This is certainly a helpful provision, but it only applies to the development of software, not to hardware, and not to the separate circumvention aids which would be needed to restore lost "fair use" or free speech abilities of normal consumers. It might be of some help in the particular case of developing a DVD player for Linux, depending on the interpretation of a number of terms and clauses.

Subsection (g) grants an exemption to subsection (a) only, for the very narrowly defined case of encryption research. The usefulness of this exception is virtually nil, as strong encryption is not readily circumvented, and weaker, circumventable encryption is of little practical or academic interest to most encryption researchers.

Subparagraph (g)(5) requires an already tardy "Report to congress" to be issued on the effects of Subsection (g). As academically interesting strong encryption is not generally used for copyright protection, this report is likely to be fairly irrelevant unless it considers the many other issues threatened by the rest of the DMCA.

Subsection (h) is a vague suggestion that it is legitimate to implement access controls which prevent minors from accessing material on the Internet. This does not appear to have any discernable legal effect.

Subsection (i) provides an exemption to subsection (a)(1) only, in a very narrow case where the consumer's privacy is being invaded by the access control and/or the copyrighted material.

$Id: dmca-guide.html,v 1.3 2000/03/27 20:27:41 niemi Exp $ 17 USC Sec 1201 01/05/1999

**Below are the notes from
http://www.tuxlaw.org/dmca/dmca-notes.txt**

"Chapter 12—Copyright Protection and Management Systems"

"Section 1201. Circumvention of copyright protection systems"

---

(a) "Violations Regarding Circumvention of Technological Measures"

(1) Circumvention of a "technological measure that effectively controls access to a work protected under this title" is prohibited after 2 years and subject to review by certain officials.

This is the second most troublesome subsection, as it appears to give any arbitrary access controls employed by a copyright holder the force of law, whether or not these access controls are reasonable, fair, or justified by legitimate business needs, or even intentional on the part of the copyright holder. It would appear that the review process indicated could, if the necessary officials were so inclined, indefinitely delay the implementation of this subsection.

The overly broad scope of this section would even seem to prohib it many routine and innocuous activites; for example, changing the permissions on a file associated with a copyrighted software program to let it be utilized under slightly different circumstances from what the copyright holder anticipated.

(2) Prohibits making pretty much any tangible item available to the public which is primarily designed or marketed for the purpose of circumventing the sort of access controls described in (a)(1).

This is by far the most troublesome provision in Section 1201. As with (a)(1) it has the problem of giving the force of law to arbitrary access controls at the whim of copyright holders. But moreover, it has no delay of implementation or review process, even if such a delay is in force for (a)(1) at the time.

Note, however, that (a)(2) does not specifically forbid providing *information* or *instructions* to the public which enable them to circumvent said access controls using commonplace items or technologies which cannot be construed to be in any way intended for the purpose of such circumvention. It would be reasonable to claim, therefore, that computer source code is such "information or instructions" which could enable (via compiling) a person to themselves create software (or another technology) which circumvents the access controls without violating (a)(2). The person actually using the "information or instructions" would then have to worry about (a)(1) if in force at that time.

(3) Definitions in support of (a)(1) and (a)(2)

(b) "Additional Violations"

(1) Identical to (a)(2) but applies to protecting the rights of a copyright holder rather than access controls.

This is not directly as bad as (a)(2), as at least it makes the pretense of requiring that the access controls have a legitimate intended purpose. However, the unintended (or worse, intended) side effects of such access controls could be just as harmful as (a)(2) above. Note that no requirement exists even in (b)(1) for there to have been any actual or even potential copyright infringement for the access controls to gain its protection; only that the access control be plausibly intended to protect copyright holder rights.

(2) Definitions in support of (b)(1)

(c) "Other Rights, Etc., Not Affected"

(1) Section 1201 does not affect normal defenses and exceptions to copyright infringement such as fair use. Note, however, that aiding someone else's otherwise legal fair use by aiding their circumvention of arbitrary access controls is not sanctioned.

(2) Section 1201 does not affect "vicarious or contributory liability for copyright infringement". Note again, that if copyright infringement (even indirect) is not involved, (c)(2) has no effect.

(3) Designers of other equipment to are not required to "provide for a response to any particular technological measure", as long as this equipment does not otherwise fall under the prohibitions of (a)(2) or (b)(1) above. It is hard to see how (c)(3) could have any useful meaning. It would seem to imply that if a subsystem of the equipment requested that access be controlled, the overall equipment would be free to ignore that request; but generally this would mean that access would be denied by the subsystem.

(4) "Nothing in this section shall enlarge or diminish any rights of free speech or the press for activities using consumer electronics, telecommunications, or computing products." It is not clear how (c)(4) in any weakens, or is even pertinent to, the stranglehold imposed by (a) and (b) above. And for that matter, the constitutional rights mentioned in (c)(4) would supersede Section 1201 in any case, so it is not actually diminishing its scope.

(d) "Exemption for Nonprofit Libraries, Archives, and Educational Institutions"

Provides a very, very narrow exemption to (a)(1), with an explicit statement that it does not provide any exemption whatsoever to (a)(2) or (b)(1).

(e) "Law Enforcement, Intelligence, and Other Government Activities"

Section 1201 does not prohibit any federal, state, or local government or their contractors from performing "any lawfully authorized investigative, protective, information security, or intelligence activity".

In theory, then, a county government could in theory claim exemption from any Section 1201 provisions as long as their actions could be justified under one of the purposes above. On the other hand, this would seem to imply that other legitimate government actions (perhaps including evaluation of products for purchase, for example) are not granted any exemption.

(f) "Reverse Engineering"

(1) An exemption to (a)(1) is granted for the extremely narrow purpose of bypassing access controls in a legally obtained computer program in order to study it in order to create a separate, interoperable program "to the extent any such acts of identification and analysis do not constitute infringement under this title".

This section shows just how overly broad sections (a)(1) and (b)(2) are. If (f)(1) were negated, arbitrary access controls could preclude all reverse engineering for compatibility purposes. Note also that (f)(1) does not appear to allow bypassing access controls which control anything other than a portion of a computer program. Finally, the last clause would seem to have the potential to negate even the narrow exemption in the rest of the paragraph.

(2) Exempts, from (a)(2) and (b)(1), technological means which aid the vanishingly narrow activities permitted by (f)(1).

However, as (a)(2) and (b)(1) do not pertain to the \*use\* of aids, but rather their distribution, (f)(2) would appear to have no immediate effect except in conjuction with (f)(3).

(3) The information gained from (f)(1) and any technological aids used in accordance with (f)(2) may be made available to others, but solely for the purpose of enabling creation of interoperable

programs, "and to the extent that doing so does not constitute infringement under this title or violate applicable law other than this section."

(f)(3) would seem like a good loophole for circumventing the dreaded (a)(2). Problems would occur if others "misused" such technological aids by using them for any other purposes than creating interoperable programs, and it is not indicated whose burden it is to ensure that such misuse does not occur. Also, the last clause would seem to negate the entire subsection, depending on the meaning of "under this title".

(g) "Encryption Research"

(1) "Definitions"

(2) "Permissible acts of encryption research"

Exemption is granted to (a)(1) for the purpose of encryption research. However, this exemption requires a great deal of the researcher, including making a "good faith effort to obtain" prior authorization.

(3) "Factors in determining exemption"

A judgement is made on the qualifications of the researcher in order for them to be permitted to use (g)(2), and the value of the research to the "state of knowledge or development of encryption technology". These factors appear to favor highly theoretical research on state-of-the-art encryption algorithms, which are not likely to be easily broken or even used to control access to copyrighted works in the first place (CSS, for example, was a very weak and poorly designed set of access controls and contained nothing of academic interest).

(4) "Use of technological means for research activities"

Exempts from (a)(2) the development and use of technical means to aid activities permitted under (g)(2) and the distribution of such aids to collaborators who are helping to conduct or verify the research activity.

Note that no exemption to (b)(1) is granted.

(5) "Report to Congress"
Requires certain officials to make a report to Congress within 1 year of passage indicating "the effect this subsection (g?) has had on:

(A) encryption research and the development of encryption technology"

(B) the adequacy and effectiveness of technological measures designed to protect copyrighted works; and

(C) protection of the copyright owners against the unauthorized access to their encrypted copyrighted works.

The report shall include legislative recommendations, if any."

Presumably the effect on (A) will be next to none as by then (a)(1) will not yet even be in force, and a single year is far too soon to have any idea how the pace of encryption research would be affected in the long run.

This report requirement also presupposes that encryption will suddenly be very widely used for protection of copyrighted works against unauthorized use. There are strong logistical and technical reasons why encryption is poorly suited to enforcing the legitimate rights of copyright holders, even in the long run. And the report is not expected to include sections about the unintended consequences of Section 1201, such as its misuse by copyright holders to gut "fair use" and to enforce arbitrary and potentially unreasonable access restrictions against the will of those who have legitimately purchased copies of their works. Nevertheless, it would be extremely interesting to find out whether such a report was actually made as required, and if so what it said.

(h) "Exceptions Regarding Minors"

A vague suggestion that it is legitimate to implement access controls which prevent minors from accessing material on the Internet.

(i) "Circumvention permitted"

Exemption to (a)(1) is permitted in the special case where the access control or the copyrighted work collects or disseminates "personally identifying information information reflecting the online activities of a natural person who seeks to gain access to the work protected" without providing conspicuous notice that it is doing so.

This exemption, as well, is quite narrow and only permits circumventing the portion of the access controls which requires the personal information.

# SERGE WROCLAWSKI
# DMCA PROTESTER
## DC Linux User Group

The issues associated with DMCA are multifaceted, but the most basic issue comes down to the control of content and the rights which were granted to the public by Fair Use. The DMCA eliminates many of those rights. This shifts the balance of power away from both the artist and the consumer and into the hands of the distributors.

I do not blame the companies for their pro-DMCA stance and their use of it in cases such as against 2600; companies are obligated to do what they feel is in their best interest. The responsibility lies in the government, whose job it is to balance the rights of individuals and the corporations, to do what is in the best interest of the nation.

## JIM GLEASON—
## President NY Linux Users Group
## Organized DMCA protests in Washington D.C.
## And in NYC.

The Digital Millenium Copyright Act is legislation that was moved through Congress by the big money lobbyists on behalf of the major motion picture studios. It was not created to protect the rights of US citizens. It is an ambiguous document that supports the interests of Hollywood and the provisions for fair use and freedom of speech have no teeth whatsoever.

Technological leaps have always caused rifts in society and industry since the beginning of time. Many people refer to the cultural change in the first half of the 1900s, when machines began to displace workers. The labor unions didn't just sit by and let that happen. They fought in the courts, they went on strike and did their best to protect their bread and butter. Did labor unions become extinct? No. Has their role diminished? Absolutely.

The MP3 music business is threatened today in the same way that DVDs are threatened by the DMCA. Within 24 hours after Napster (the free distribution music web site) was shutdown on 7/27/00, 1.2 million people fled to Gnutella, (a network of systems devoted to file-sharing software) to get freely distributed music. This is a lot consumers! Clearly, market demand in the music industry is changing. The rock group Metallica and the big record companies represented by their lobbyists at the RIAA, are very worried about these implications.

Stephen King is writing an online book called "The Plant" in which he is receiving $1 for every chapter he writes from Internet users who want him to finish the book. Payment is on the honor system, but by the end of the first day (7/24/00), he received $93,200 in credit card payments from Amazon.com. King proclaims that that he only had to invest $124,150 to get the project going! He expects to write at least ten chapters! Needless to say, the publishing industry is extremely distressed. Ironically, the story is about a "vampire" vine that terrorizes a small publishing house.

These events provide valuable frontline information about how the customer base for entertainment products is evolving. Universal Studios, via their lobbyists at the MPAA, are trying to prevent this cultural evolution from happening by passing laws like the DMCA. They think they can legally stop their customer base from investigating and invigorating this new form of expression.

Filmmakers, musicians, authors and all of the other owners of entertainment properties will learn how to get customers directly via the Internet much more quickly than the movie studios, the record labels and the publishing houses. This will take a few years, but the artists themselves have much more economic motivation to do this than the established entertainment industry. It's easy to forsee a day when artists will create their own collectives to share production resources and split revenues.

When this happens, the DMCA will be forgotten and become irrelevant. My prediction is that the movie studios will ultimately sell the ownership of their aging properties to the American Movie Classics cable channel—the last stop for old movies.

—Jim

# TIMOTHY LORD
# WRITER
# DMCA PROTESTER
# SLASHDOT.ORG

**Taken with permission from a conversation with Timothy Lord (verifiable) in irc.linux.com**

oh, the DMCA is an invasive, poorly considered law.

By making it illegal to sidestep even trivial encryption, the DMCA grants to copyright holders unprecedented power....and grants special power to current copyright holding industry groups.

It also destroys vital freedoms with regard to education by attempting to define and delimite "legitimate" research as that done only by approved institutions.
(wrt to reverse engineering and crypto tools)

By placing a burden of proof on those who would examine software running on their own computers, it provides a layer of protection to established software vendors and other content providers more appropriate to a mercantalist econony than a free one.

**Author's note: wrt = With Regard To**

# JOHN YOUNG
# OPENLAW PARTICIPANT
# ARCHIVIST
# CRYPTOME.ORG

The DMCA must be interpreted, or revised, to allow greatest freedom for researchers to investigate digital inventions and products. Without such freedom creative advancement will be inhibited, or worse, will be forced to take place only for commercial purposes, or worst of all, under illegal conditions.

There can be no greater harm to fostering and protecting creative endeavor than to force compliance with provisions developed by the copyright industry.


John Young

# EMMETT PLANT
## Former Slashdot Author
## and
## Editor-in-Chief of Linux.com

The DMCA is a victim of the times. Unfortunately, property is nine-tenths of the law, and work under the DMCA becomes a much more tangible property. I think one of the reasons for this is because for years and years, we considered 'property' to be tangible things. A house and the land it sits on. Your new car. Your mother's fine china.

Now we live in a world where property takes on entirely new and beautiful connotations. Your mother's fine china has a patina. One of my songs that I distribute online has more than just a bass line and a wailing accordion, it also has an intrinsic quality in being a digital sound file. Our songs, our words, have wings. A lot of musicians and writers have decided to waive their rights to support and foster these new qualities. We're making the beautiful patina of your mother's china available to anyone in the world for free.

This is not an easy concept to grasp, especially to a large group of lawyers who have been dealing with real property for most of their lives, and only have access to massive libraries filled with information from other lawyers that have been dealing with real property for most of their lives. Lawmakers have no reason to investigate the new market; they tend to get paid no matter what. It is unfortunate that the concepts and meanings behind the DMCA juggernaut can't be broken down to political catch-phrases like 'Just say no,' or 'Read my lips, no new taxes.' Then again, maybe they can. 'Don't tread on me.'

## DON MARTI
## TECHNICAL EDITOR
## LINUXJOURNAL
### Member Silicon Valley LUGS

DMCA makes the Communications Decency Act look like a parking ticket. By banning the circumvention of access control measures, DMCA indirectly bans many legitimate personal, educational, and political uses of important information.

DMCA enables a corporation to conceal information about software that makes a political decision to censor information. Last year, the company that owns the Internet censorship program "Cyber Patrol" sued two encryption experts who analyzed the list of web sites that Cyber Patrol blocks. The experts published a paper documenting the alarming fact that Cyber Patrol, at the time, blocked sites opposed to nuclear weapons — including the Nuclear Control Institute and part of the City of Hiroshima web site.

But because of DMCA, the paper was suppressed. Cyber Patrol has used DMCA to defend its privatized, secret censorship of public facilities including libraries and schools.

In many cases, the "access control" measures protected by DMCA have nothing to do with preventing copying and everything to do with asserting unprecedented corporate control over the user. I am confident that the Supreme Court will throw DMCA out.

— Don Marti No haiku patents
…Software patent reform now: <*http://burnallgifs.org/*>

# BRYAN TAYLOR
# OPENLAW

The Digitial Millenium Copyright Act is a perfect example of how a good idea can turn bad, very bad, when special interests and corporate greed exert their influence on the political process. The original idea of the DMCA is reasonable enough: allow authors to have a new payment scheme for profiting from their works. This scheme would allow them to sell encryption keys instead of hardcopy and facilitate an alternative for commerce of copyrighted material, especially over the internet.

The problem is that the current political reality in Washington and across the Country got in the way. To be blunt, Congressmen have to suck up to monied interests to survive.

When Big Money wants to eliminate bothersome things that interfere with their ability to maximize profits, the public interst, science, consumer rights, even First Amendment rights, are swept aside. The enormous sums of funding that one must raise to effectively campaign today force this result, and have been at work for years already, so that Congress is full of people who can feel good about themselves for "promoting commerce" even as they trample on everything else American's hold dear.

So it was with the DMCA. The good idea became the fifteen second talking point that covered for the sinister alterior motive. The real goal of the DMCA, of course, is to eliminate the Constitutional barriers inherent in intellectual property law that run counter to maximizing profit. Nevermind that the Supreme Court has said repeatedly that the Constitutional purpose of the Copyright Clause is to promote the progress of science and the useful arts and that profit to the copyright holder is a secondary consideration.

The DMCA was written to provide absolute control of encrypted content. You exercise this control by creating a "technological protection measure", and the DMCA grants you a monopoly over "access" to the encrypted content. Fair use of encrypted content is abolished. The first sale right to display copyrighted material you own to others in your presense (or even yourself) also is abolished. The First Amendment right to tell other people factual details of how the protection measures work is abolished. The incredibile nullification machine called the DMCA does not care about such things because they get in the way of corporate profit.

The big three "Copyright Industries" (music, movies, software) lobbied heavily for passage of the DMCA. Jack Valenti, head of the MPAA, literally swore under oath that he had no idea how many times he has testified before Congress. If that is not a clue to the excessive influence of big buisiness in today's politics, then I don't know what is.

Scientists, engineers, librarians, and civil liberties groups rallied to oppose the DMCA. They were thrown a few crumbs. President Clinton signed the bill into law in October of 1998. Hollywood has given millions of dollars to the democratic party and Clinton's campaign.

With two of the three branches of government corrupted, it didn't take long for a review of the DMCA to wind up before the judiciary, the protector of freedom, the one group that is supposed to be above politics. Well, Federal District Judge Lewis Kaplan, appointed by Bill Clinton for his meritorious service as an antitrust lawyer defending big corporations including Warner Brothers, recently upheld the DMCA when it was challenged by a group that had posted a utility used to decrypt DVD's so they could be watched under Linux. The judge's partner was even helping Warner Brothers with it's DVD antitrust positioning in the months leading to Kaplan's appointment to the bench. The judge denied the motion requesting that he recuse himself.

There are two steps left before the final verdict. The Second Circuit Court of Appeals may reverse, or the Supreme Court might decide to take the case and reverse. I am hopeful that one of the two will happen, but it is by no means a sure thing. Even if the DMCA is struck down, the conditions that create it remain. It is time to reverse the undue influence of big money in politics.

# MATTHEW SKALA
# CP4Break/CPHack

Fundamentally, the DMCA says that you don't own your property anymore. If a corporation sells or gives you something, the corporation still owns it and can set arbitrary rules on how you may use it. That's bad enough in the case of intangibles like software. It perverts the original purpose of copyright which was to encourage the release of material into the public domain by offering artists a temporary, limited, and artificial monopoly on their work. But the anti-circumvention clause applying to hardware makes it even worse, because it allows the manufacturer to sell you a machine while setting arbitrary limits on how you may or may not use it, with the force of criminal law backing those limits. Imagine a car that not only would stop working if you drove past a competing dealership, but with a squad of police ready to arrest you as soon as you tried. Literally, you do not own your property anymore.

Matthew Skala *mskala@xxxxx.xxxxx.xx.xx* I'm recording the boycott industry! *http://www.islandnet.com/~mskala/*

# WENDY SELZER
# OPENLAW
**Fellow, Berkman Center for Internet & Society at Harvard Law School**

Paradoxically, at just the time when the success of open source software is showing the value to be gained from free and open exchange of information, publishers and lawmakers are restricting those exchanges in the name of protections for intellectual property. As the GNU/Linux operating system gains in popularity, publishers claim it is illegal to play their movies on the computers it operates. By imposing and enforcing "access controls" to limit the use of published media, these publishers tip the balance in which copyright was conceived, no longer "to promote the progress of science and useful arts."

Section 1201 of the Digital Millennium Copyright Act ("DMCA"), the anticircumvention provision, grants a novel right of "access control" to publishers. When a copyright owner applies a technological measure, even a trivially simple encryption scheme, to its work, 1201 makes it illegal to use even a purchased copy of that work in a manner it has not explicitly approved. Publishers are already using such technological controls in attempts to remove published works beyond the reach of discussion, criticism, and other fair uses, saying the purchaser is granted "access" to only to view. They seek through technology to abrogate decades of judicial balancing between copy control and public access.

The American framers understood copyright as a necessary evil, granting a limited monopoly to authors to encourage them to publish and disseminate works. Instead of publication, however, the anticircumvention provision encourages "privacation," a strange hybrid in which publishers sell copies of their works to the public wthout giving them full rights to view or use those copies. With the help of the DMCA, the publishing industries are pushing us toward "trusted systems," encrypted media and devices that will play those media only in the limited ways the publisher dictates. The result is music you may not lend, DVDs you cannot fast-forward through commercials, books you cannot quote for criticism, and works you do not own but pay-per-view. Moreover, these restrictions may be the only terms on which the work is available.

The "trust" in trusted systems is not with the public user, but only with a player device that is heavily shielded from user investigation. Under recent judicial interpretations, to build your own player for protected media without the approval of the copyright owner is to "circumvent" the access controls in violation of Section 1201. Not only are the copyrighted works thus locked away from fair uses, but discussion of the player devices and their operation is prohibited "trafficking" in circumvention tools. Instead of openly shared information and publicly accessible works, the DMCA fosters proprietary data and proprietary formats. Anticircumvention is anti-research, anti-tinkering, and anti-innovation. Indeed, Section 1201 threatens open source development because, in its inverted sense, a trusted system's "trust" is compromised by source code availability. Interoperability is sacrificed to the hyper-protection of intellectual content.

It seems eons ago, in Internet time, that we were speaking of the potential of the "Information Superhighway" for information exchange. Notwithstanding the fears of current publishers more concerned about preserving their business models than the balance of copyright, we must recognize intellectual property still gains in value by being shared. We fight the protectionist stance of anticircumvention to preserve these avenues of information exchange.

# GERALD THURMAN
**Educator**
**CSE/CIS Instructor**

I have not delivered your DCMA comment because I don't understand legal stuff; I don't like legal stuff; I try to avoid getting involved in legal stuff.

Curiously, I have not be able to easily find information about it. I wanted to read the opionions of Richard Stallman and Ed Yourdon on the Act, but I couldn't find them in a timely fashion. [I did however find time to look at Stallman's pictures from a trip he took to China.]

To me the Act violates the Unix Philosophy and is way too broad. Tries to address too many topics that are part of the system, but their interfaces are completely undefined.

It talks about computer criminal activity that implies security measures are built into tools. Major concern is the allowing of hooks to be incorporated into tools—typically these hooks suck and are cracked.

Too me there have not been enough Internet issues resolved in the courts. Many that are, are often found to have defects. There is a saying in computing that goes: You Want It Bad, You Get It Bad [GuyT—printed without permission].

I think DMCA is worthy of more study, discussion, and editing, but it should not have been shipped.

G.D.Thurman [CS/CIS Instructor]

From:      Josef Robey <josef@napster.com> Wed, 27 Sep 2000
            10:51:30 -0700

Subject:   FW: Fwd: DMCA comment/opinion

To:         "'marcia@linuxstart.com'"

We don't have a specific comment, but we do discuss DMCA in our legal papers.

Please see: *http://www.napster.com/pressroom/legal.html*

Thanks

# Appendix III
# DMCA

*ftp://ftp.loc.gov/pub/thomas/cp105/hr796.txt* (report)

Full Text of the DMCA

*http://www.hrrc.org/H.R._2281-_final_text.pdf*

---

H.R.2281

## One Hundred Fifth Congress
## of the
## United States of America
## AT THE SECOND SESSION

Begun and held at the City of Washington on Tuesday, the twenty-seventh day of January, one thousand nine hundred and ninety-eight

## An Act

To amend title 17, United States Code, to implement the World Intellectual Property Organization Copyright Treaty and Performances and Phonograms Treaty, and for other purposes.

*Be it enacted by the Senate and House of Representatives of the United States of America in Congress assembled,*

## SECTION 1. SHORT TITLE.

This Act may be cited as the 'Digital Millennium Copyright Act'.

## SEC. 2. TABLE OF CONTENTS.

## TITLE III—COMPUTER MAINTENANCE OR REPAIR COPYRIGHT EXEMPTION

Sec. 301. Short title.

Sec. 302. Limitations on exclusive rights; computer programs.

## TITLE IV—MISCELLANEOUS PROVISIONS

Sec. 401. Provisions Relating to the Commissioner of Patents and Trademarks and the Register of Copyrights.

Sec. 402. Ephemeral recordings.

Sec. 403. Limitations on exclusive rights; distance education.

Sec. 404. Exemption for libraries and archives.

Sec. 405. Scope of exclusive rights in sound recordings; ephemeral recordings.

Sec. 406. Assumption of contractual obligations related to transfers of rights in motion pictures.

Sec. 407. Effective date.

## TITLE V—PROTECTION OF CERTAIN ORIGINAL DESIGNS

Sec. 501. Short title.

Sec. 502. Protection of certain original designs.

Sec. 503. Conforming amendments.

Sec. 504. Joint study of the effect of this title.

Sec. 505. Effective date.

## TITLE I—WIPO TREATIES IMPLEMENTATION

## SEC. 101. SHORT TITLE.

This title may be cited as the 'WIPO Copyright and Performances and Phonograms Treaties Implementation Act of 1998'.

## SEC. 102. TECHNICAL AMENDMENTS.

(a) DEFINITIONS- Section 101 of title 17, United States Code, is amended—

(1) by striking the definition of 'Berne Convention work';

(2) in the definition of 'The 'country of origin' of a Berne Convention work'—

> (A) by striking 'The 'country of origin' of a Berne Convention work, for purposes of section 411, is the United States if' and inserting 'For purposes of section 411, a work is a 'United States work' only if';
>
> (B) in paragraph (1)—
>
>> (i) in subparagraph (B) by striking 'nation or nations adhering to the Berne Convention' and inserting 'treaty party or parties';
>>
>> (ii) in subparagraph (C) by striking 'does not adhere to the Berne Convention' and inserting 'is not a treaty party'; and

(iii) in subparagraph (D) by striking 'does not adhere to the Berne Convention' and inserting 'is not a treaty party'; and

(C) in the matter following paragraph (3) by striking 'For the purposes of section 411, the 'country of origin' of any other Berne Convention work is not the United States.';

(3) by inserting after the definition of 'fixed' the following:

'The 'Geneva Phonograms Convention' is the Convention for the Protection of Producers of Phonograms Against Unauthorized Duplication of Their Phonograms, concluded at Geneva, Switzerland, on October 29, 1971.';

(4) by inserting after the definition of 'including' the following:

'An 'international agreement' is—

'(1) the Universal Copyright Convention;

'(2) the Geneva Phonograms Convention;

'(3) the Berne Convention;

'(4) the WTO Agreement;

'(5) the WIPO Copyright Treaty;

'(6) the WIPO Performances and Phonograms Treaty; and

'(7) any other copyright treaty to which the United States is a party.';

(5) by inserting after the definition of 'transmit' the following:

'A 'treaty party' is a country or intergovernmental organization other than the United States that is a party to an international agreement.';

(6) by inserting after the definition of 'widow' the following:

'The 'WIPO Copyright Treaty' is the WIPO Copyright Treaty concluded at Geneva, Switzerland, on December 20, 1996.';

(7) by inserting after the definition of 'The 'WIPO Copyright Treaty' the following:

'The 'WIPO Performances and Phonograms Treaty' is the WIPO Performances and Phonograms Treaty concluded at Geneva, Switzerland, on December 20, 1996.'; and

(8) by inserting after the definition of 'work made for hire' the following:

'The terms 'WTO Agreement' and 'WTO member country' have the meanings given those terms in paragraphs (9) and (10), respectively, of section 2 of the Uruguay Round Agreements Act.'.

(b) SUBJECT MATTER OF COPYRIGHT; NATIONAL ORIGIN-Section 104 of title 17, United States Code, is amended—

(1) in subsection (b)—

(A) in paragraph (1) by striking 'foreign nation that is a party to a copyright treaty to which the United States is also a party' and inserting 'treaty party';

(B) in paragraph (2) by striking 'party to the Universal Copyright Convention' and inserting 'treaty party';

(C) by redesignating paragraph (5) as paragraph (6);

(D) by redesignating paragraph (3) as paragraph (5) and inserting it after paragraph (4);

(E) by inserting after paragraph (2) the following:

'(3) the work is a sound recording that was first fixed in a treaty party; or';

(F) in paragraph (4) by striking 'Berne Convention work' and inserting 'pictorial, graphic, or sculptural work that is incorporated in a building or other structure, or an architectural work that is embodied in a building and the building or structure is located in the United States or a treaty party'; and

(G) by inserting after paragraph (6), as so redesignated, the following:

'For purposes of paragraph (2), a work that is published in the United States or a treaty party within 30 days after publication in a foreign nation that is not a treaty party shall be considered to be first published in the United States or such treaty party, as the case may be.'; and

(2) by adding at the end the following new subsection:

'(d) EFFECT OF PHONOGRAMS TREATIES- Notwithstanding the provisions of subsection (b), no works other than sound recordings shall be eligible for protection under this title solely by virtue of the adherence of the United States to the Geneva Phonograms Convention or the WIPO Performances and Phonograms Treaty.'.

(c) COPYRIGHT IN RESTORED WORKS- Section 104A(h) of title 17, United States Code, is amended—

(1) in paragraph (1), by striking subparagraphs (A) and (B) and inserting the following:

'(A) a nation adhering to the Berne Convention;

'(B) a WTO member country;

'(C) a nation adhering to the WIPO Copyright Treaty;

'(D) a nation adhering to the WIPO Performances and Phonograms Treaty; or

'(E) subject to a Presidential proclamation under subsection (g).';

(2) by amending paragraph (3) to read as follows:

'(3) The term 'eligible country' means a nation, other than the United States, that—

'(A) becomes a WTO member country after the date of the enactment of the Uruguay Round Agreements Act;

'(B) on such date of enactment is, or after such date of enactment becomes, a nation adhering to the Berne Convention;

'(C) adheres to the WIPO Copyright Treaty;

'(D) adheres to the WIPO Performances and Phonograms Treaty; or

'(E) after such date of enactment becomes subject to a proclamation under subsection (g).';

(3) in paragraph (6)—

(A) in subparagraph (C)(iii) by striking 'and' after the semi-colon;

(B) at the end of subparagraph (D) by striking the period and inserting '; and'; and

(C) by adding after subparagraph (D) the following:

'(E) if the source country for the work is an eligible country solely by virtue of its adherence to the WIPO Performances and Phonograms Treaty, is a sound recording.';

(4) in paragraph (8)(B)(i)—

(A) by inserting 'of which' before 'the majority'; and

(B) by striking 'of eligible countries'; and

(5) by striking paragraph (9).

(d) REGISTRATION AND INFRINGEMENT ACTIONS- Section 411(a) of title 17, United States Code, is amended in the first sentence—

(1) by striking 'actions for infringement of copyright in Berne Convention works whose country of origin is not the United States and'; and

(2) by inserting 'United States' after 'no action for infringement of the copyright in any'.

(e) STATUTE OF LIMITATIONS- Section 507(a) of title 17, United State Code, is amended by striking 'No' and inserting 'Except as expressly provided otherwise in this title, no'.

## SEC. 103. COPYRIGHT PROTECTION SYSTEMS AND COPYRIGHT MANAGEMENT INFORMATION.

(a) IN GENERAL- Title 17, United States Code, is amended by adding at the end the following new chapter:

# 'CHAPTER 12—COPYRIGHT PROTECTION AND MANAGEMENT SYSTEMS

'Sec.

'1201. Circumvention of copyright protection systems.

'1202. Integrity of copyright management information.

'1203. Civil remedies.

'1204. Criminal offenses and penalties.

'1205. Savings clause.

### 'Sec. 1201. Circumvention of copyright protection systems

'(a) VIOLATIONS REGARDING CIRCUMVENTION OF TECHNOLOGICAL MEASURES- (1)(A) No person shall circumvent a technological measure that effectively controls access to a work protected under this title. The prohibition contained in the preceding sentence shall take effect at the end of the 2-year period beginning on the date of the enactment of this chapter.

'(B) The prohibition contained in subparagraph (A) shall not apply to persons who are users of a copyrighted work which is in a particular class of works, if such persons are, or are likely to be in the succeeding 3-year period, adversely affected by virtue of such prohibition in their ability to make noninfringing uses of that particular class of works under this title, as determined under subparagraph (C).

'(C) During the 2-year period described in subparagraph (A), and during each succeeding 3-year period, the Librarian of Congress, upon the recommendation of the Register of Copyrights, who shall consult with the Assistant Secretary for Communications and Information of the Department of Commerce and report and comment on his or her views in making such recommendation, shall make the determination in a rulemaking proceeding on the record for purposes of subparagraph (B) of whether persons who are users of a copyrighted work are, or are likely to be in the succeeding 3-year period, adversely affected by the prohibition under subparagraph (A) in their ability to make noninfringing uses under this title of a particular class of copyrighted works. In conducting such rulemaking, the Librarian shall examine—

'(i) the availability for use of copyrighted works;

'(ii) the availability for use of works for nonprofit archival, preservation, and educational purposes;

'(iii) the impact that the prohibition on the circumvention of technological measures applied to copyrighted works has on criticism, comment, news reporting, teaching, scholarship, or research;

'(iv) the effect of circumvention of technological measures on the market for or value of copyrighted works; and

'(v) such other factors as the Librarian considers appropriate.

'(D) The Librarian shall publish any class of copyrighted works for which the Librarian has determined, pursuant to the rulemaking conducted under subparagraph (C), that noninfringing uses by persons who are users of a copyrighted work are, or are likely to be, adversely affected, and the prohibition contained in subparagraph (A) shall not apply to such users with respect to such class of works for the ensuing 3-year period.

'(E) Neither the exception under subparagraph (B) from the applicability of the prohibition contained in subparagraph (A), nor any determination made in a rulemaking conducted under subparagraph (C), may be used as a defense in any action to enforce any provision of this title other than this paragraph.

'(2) No person shall manufacture, import, offer to the public, provide, or otherwise traffic in any technology, product, service, device, component, or part thereof, that—

'(A) is primarily designed or produced for the purpose of circumventing a technological measure that effectively controls access to a work protected under this title;

'(B) has only limited commercially significant purpose or use other than to circumvent a technological measure that effectively controls access to a work protected under this title; or

'(C) is marketed by that person or another acting in concert with that person with that person's knowledge for use in circumventing a technological measure that effectively controls access to a work protected under this title.

'(3) As used in this subsection—

'(A) to 'circumvent a technological measure' means to descramble a scrambled work, to decrypt an encrypted work, or otherwise to avoid, bypass, remove, deactivate, or impair a technological measure, without the authority of the copyright owner; and

'(B) a technological measure 'effectively controls access to a work' if the measure, in the ordinary course of its operation, requires the application of information, or a process or a treatment, with the authority of the copyright owner, to gain access to the work.

'(b) ADDITIONAL VIOLATIONS- (1) No person shall manufacture, import, offer to the public, provide, or otherwise traffic in any technology, product, service, device, component, or part thereof, that—

'(A) is primarily designed or produced for the purpose of circumventing protection afforded by a technological measure that effectively protects a right of a copyright owner under this title in a work or a portion thereof;

'(B) has only limited commercially significant purpose or use other than to circumvent protection afforded by a technological measure that effectively protects a right of a copyright owner under this title in a work or a portion thereof; or

'(C) is marketed by that person or another acting in concert with that person with that person's knowledge for use in circumventing protection afforded by a technological measure that effectively protects a right of a copyright owner under this title in a work or a portion thereof.

'(2) As used in this subsection—

'(A) to 'circumvent protection afforded by a technological measure' means avoiding, bypassing, removing, deactivating, or otherwise impairing a technological measure; and

'(B) a technological measure 'effectively protects a right of a copyright owner under this title' if the measure, in the ordinary course of its operation, prevents, restricts, or otherwise limits the exercise of a right of a copyright owner under this title.

'(c) OTHER RIGHTS, ETC., NOT AFFECTED- (1) Nothing in this section shall affect rights, remedies, limitations, or defenses to copyright infringement, including fair use, under this title.

'(2) Nothing in this section shall enlarge or diminish vicarious or contributory liability for copyright infringement in connection with any technology, product, service, device, component, or part thereof.

'(3) Nothing in this section shall require that the design of, or design and selection of parts and components for, a consumer electronics, telecommunications, or computing product provide for a response to any particular technological measure, so long as such part or component, or the product in which such part or component is integrated, does not otherwise fall within the prohibitions of subsection (a)(2) or (b)(1).

'(4) Nothing in this section shall enlarge or diminish any rights of free speech or the press for activities using consumer electronics, telecommunications, or computing products.

'(d) EXEMPTION FOR NONPROFIT LIBRARIES, ARCHIVES, AND EDUCATIONAL INSTITUTIONS- (1) A nonprofit library, archives, or educational institution which gains access to a commercially exploited copyrighted work solely in order to make a good faith determination of whether to acquire a copy of that work for the sole purpose of engaging in conduct permitted under this title shall not be in violation of subsection (a)(1)(A). A copy of a work to which access has been gained under this paragraph—

'(A) may not be retained longer than necessary to make such good faith determination; and

'(B) may not be used for any other purpose.

'(2) The exemption made available under paragraph (1) shall only apply with respect to a work when an identical copy of that work is not reasonably available in another form.

'(3) A nonprofit library, archives, or educational institution that willfully for the purpose of commercial advantage or financial gain violates paragraph (1)—

'(A) shall, for the first offense, be subject to the civil remedies under section 1203; and

'(B) shall, for repeated or subsequent offenses, in addition to the civil remedies under section 1203, forfeit the exemption provided under paragraph (1).

'(4) This subsection may not be used as a defense to a claim under subsection (a)(2) or (b), nor may this subsection permit a nonprofit library, archives, or educational institution to manufacture, import, offer to the public, provide, or otherwise traffic in any technology, product, service, component, or part thereof, which circumvents a technological measure.

'(5) In order for a library or archives to qualify for the exemption under this subsection, the collections of that library or archives shall be—

'(A) open to the public; or

'(B) available not only to researchers affiliated with the library or archives or with the institution of which it is a part, but also to other persons doing research in a specialized field.

'(e) LAW ENFORCEMENT, INTELLIGENCE, AND OTHER GOVERNMENT ACTIVITIES- This section does not prohibit any lawfully authorized investigative, protective, information security, or intelligence activity of an officer, agent, or employee of the United States, a State, or a political subdivision of a State, or a person acting pursuant to a contract with the United States, a State, or a political subdivision of a State. For purposes of this subsection, the term 'information security' means activities carried out in order to identify and address the vulnerabilities of a government computer, computer system, or computer network.

'(f) REVERSE ENGINEERING- (1) Notwithstanding the provisions of subsection (a)(1)(A), a person who has lawfully obtained the right to use a copy of a computer program may circumvent a technological measure that effectively controls access to a particular portion of that program for the sole purpose of identifying and analyzing those elements of the program that are necessary to achieve interoperability of an independently created computer program with other programs, and that have not previously been readily available to the person engaging in the circumvention, to the extent any such acts of identification and analysis do not constitute infringement under this title.

'(2) Notwithstanding the provisions of subsections (a)(2) and (b), a person may develop and employ technological means to circumvent a technological measure, or to circumvent protection afforded by a technological measure, in order to enable the identification and analysis under paragraph (1), or for the purpose of enabling interoperability of an independently created computer program with other programs, if such means are necessary to achieve such interoperability, to the extent that doing so does not constitute infringement under this title.

'(3) The information acquired through the acts permitted under paragraph (1), and the means permitted under paragraph (2), may be made available to others if the person referred to in paragraph (1) or (2), as the case may be, provides such information or means solely for the purpose of enabling interoperability of an independently created computer program with other programs, and to the extent that doing so does not constitute infringement under this title or violate applicable law other than this section.

'(4) For purposes of this subsection, the term 'interoperability' means the ability of computer programs to exchange information, and of such programs mutually to use the information which has been exchanged.

'(g) ENCRYPTION RESEARCH-

'(1) DEFINITIONS- For purposes of this subsection—

'(A) the term 'encryption research' means activities necessary to identify and analyze flaws and vulnerabilities of encryption technologies applied to copyrighted works, if these activities are conducted to advance the state of knowledge in the field of encryption technology or to assist in the development of encryption products; and

'(B) the term 'encryption technology' means the scrambling and descrambling of information using mathematical formulas or algorithms.

'(2) PERMISSIBLE ACTS OF ENCRYPTION RESEARCH- Notwithstanding the provisions of subsection (a)(1)(A), it is not a violation of that subsection for a person to circumvent a technological measure as applied to a copy, phonorecord, performance, or display of a published work in the course of an act of good faith encryption research if—

'(A) the person lawfully obtained the encrypted copy, phonorecord, performance, or display of the published work;

'(B) such act is necessary to conduct such encryption research;

'(C) the person made a good faith effort to obtain authorization before the circumvention; and

'(D) such act does not constitute infringement under this title or a violation of applicable law other than this section, including section 1030 of title 18 and those provisions of title 18 amended by the Computer Fraud and Abuse Act of 1986.

'(3) FACTORS IN DETERMINING EXEMPTION- In determining whether a person qualifies for the exemption under paragraph (2), the factors to be considered shall include—

'(A) whether the information derived from the encryption research was disseminated, and if so, whether it was disseminated in a manner reasonably calculated to advance the state of knowledge or development of encryption technology, versus whether it was disseminated in a manner that facilitates infringement under this title or a violation of applicable law other than this section, including a violation of privacy or breach of security;

'(B) whether the person is engaged in a legitimate course of study, is employed, or is appropriately trained or experienced, in the field of encryption technology; and

'(C) whether the person provides the copyright owner of the work to which the technological measure is applied with notice of the findings and documentation of the research, and the time when such notice is provided.

'(4) USE OF TECHNOLOGICAL MEANS FOR RESEARCH ACTIVITIES- Notwithstanding the provisions of subsection (a)(2), it is not a violation of that subsection for a person to—

'(A) develop and employ technological means to circumvent a technological measure for the sole purpose of that person performing the acts of good faith encryption research described in paragraph (2); and

'(B) provide the technological means to another person with whom he or she is working collaboratively for the purpose of conducting the acts of good faith encryption research described in paragraph (2) or for the purpose of having that other person verify his or her acts of good faith encryption research described in paragraph (2).

'(5) REPORT TO CONGRESS- Not later than 1 year after the date of the enactment of this chapter, the Register of Copyrights and the Assistant Secretary for Communications and Information of the Department of Commerce shall jointly report to the Congress on the effect this subsection has had on—

'(A) encryption research and the development of encryption technology;

'(B) the adequacy and effectiveness of technological measures designed to protect copyrighted works; and

'(C) protection of copyright owners against the unauthorized access to their encrypted copyrighted works.

The report shall include legislative recommendations, if any.

'(h) EXCEPTIONS REGARDING MINORS- In applying subsection (a) to a component or part, the court may consider the necessity for its intended and actual incorporation in a technology, product, service, or device, which—

'(1) does not itself violate the provisions of this title; and

'(2) has the sole purpose to prevent the access of minors to material on the Internet.

'(i) PROTECTION OF PERSONALLY IDENTIFYING INFORMATION-

(1) CIRCUMVENTION PERMITTED- Notwithstanding the provisions of subsection (a)(1)(A), it is not a violation of that subsection for a person to circumvent a technological measure that effectively controls access to a work protected under this title, if—

'(A) the technological measure, or the work it protects, contains the capability of collecting or disseminating personally identifying information reflecting the online activities of a natural person who seeks to gain access to the work protected;

'(B) in the normal course of its operation, the technological measure, or the work it protects, collects or disseminates personally identifying information about the person who seeks to gain access to the work protected, without providing conspicuous notice of such collection or dissemination to such person, and without providing such person with the capability to prevent or restrict such collection or dissemination;

'(C) the act of circumvention has the sole effect of identifying and disabling the capability described in subparagraph (A), and has no other effect on the ability of any person to gain access to any work; and

'(D) the act of circumvention is carried out solely for the purpose of preventing the collection or dissemination of personally identifying information about a natural person who seeks to gain access to the work protected, and is not in violation of any other law.

'(2) INAPPLICABILITY TO CERTAIN TECHNOLOGICAL MEASURES- This subsection does not apply to a technological measure, or a work it protects, that does not collect or disseminate personally identifying information and that is disclosed to a user as not having or using such capability.

'(j) SECURITY TESTING-

'(1) DEFINITION- For purposes of this subsection, the term 'security testing' means accessing a computer, computer system, or computer network, solely for the purpose of good faith testing, investigating, or correcting, a security flaw or vulnerability, with the authorization of the owner or operator of such computer, computer system, or computer network.

'(2) PERMISSIBLE ACTS OF SECURITY TESTING- Notwithstanding the provisions of subsection (a)(1)(A), it is not a violation of that subsection for a person to engage in an act of security testing, if such act does not constitute infringement under this title or a violation of applicable law other than this section, including section 1030 of title 18 and those provisions of title 18 amended by the Computer Fraud and Abuse Act of 1986.

'(3) FACTORS IN DETERMINING EXEMPTION- In determining whether a person qualifies for the exemption under paragraph (2), the factors to be considered shall include—

'(A) whether the information derived from the security testing was used solely to promote the security of the owner or operator of such computer, computer system or computer network, or shared directly with the developer of such computer, computer system, or computer network; and

'(B) whether the information derived from the security testing was used or maintained in a manner that does not facilitate infringement under this title or a violation of applicable law other than this section, including a violation of privacy or breach of security.

'(4) USE OF TECHNOLOGICAL MEANS FOR SECURITY TESTING- Notwithstanding the provisions of subsection (a)(2), it is not a violation of that subsection for a person to develop, produce, distribute or employ technological means for the sole purpose of performing the acts of security testing described in subsection (2), provided such technological means does not otherwise violate section (a)(2).

'(k) CERTAIN ANALOG DEVICES AND CERTAIN TECHNOLOGICAL MEASURES-

'(1) CERTAIN ANALOG DEVICES-

'(A) Effective 18 months after the date of the enactment of this chapter, no person shall manufacture, import, offer to the public, provide or otherwise traffic in any—

'(i) VHS format analog video cassette recorder unless such recorder conforms to the automatic gain control copy control technology;

'(ii) 8mm format analog video cassette camcorder unless such camcorder conforms to the automatic gain control technology;

'(iii) Beta format analog video cassette recorder, unless such recorder conforms to the automatic gain control copy control technology, except that this requirement shall not apply until there are 1,000 Beta format analog video cassette recorders sold in the United States in any one calendar year after the date of the enactment of this chapter;

'(iv) 8mm format analog video cassette recorder that is not an analog video cassette camcorder, unless such recorder conforms to the automatic gain control copy control technology, except that this requirement shall not apply until there are 20,000 such recorders sold in the United States in any one calendar year after the date of the enactment of this chapter; or

'(v) analog video cassette recorder that records using an NTSC format video input and that is not otherwise covered under clauses (i) through (iv), unless such device conforms to the automatic gain control copy control technology.

'(B) Effective on the date of the enactment of this chapter, no person shall manufacture, import, offer to the public, provide or otherwise traffic in—

'(i) any VHS format analog video cassette recorder or any 8mm format analog video cassette recorder if the design of the model of such recorder has been modified after such date of enactment so that a model of recorder that previously conformed to the automatic gain control copy control technology no longer conforms to such technology; or

'(ii) any VHS format analog video cassette recorder, or any 8mm format analog video cassette recorder that is not an 8mm analog video cassette camcorder, if the design of the model of such recorder has been modified after such date of enactment so that a model of recorder that previously conformed to the four-line colorstripe copy control technology no longer conforms to such technology.

Manufacturers that have not previously manufactured or sold a VHS format analog video cassette recorder, or an 8mm format analog cassette recorder, shall be required to conform to the four-line colorstripe copy control technology in the initial model of any such recorder manufactured after the date of the enactment of this chapter, and thereafter to continue conforming to the four-line colorstripe copy control technology. For purposes of this subparagraph, an analog video cassette recorder 'conforms to' the four-line colorstripe copy control technology if it records a signal that, when played back by the playback function of that recorder in the normal viewing mode, exhibits, on a reference display device, a display containing distracting visible lines through portions of the viewable picture.

'(2) CERTAIN ENCODING RESTRICTIONS- No person shall apply the automatic gain control copy control technology or colorstripe copy control technology to prevent or limit consumer copying except such copying—

'(A) of a single transmission, or specified group of transmissions, of live events or of audiovisual works for which a member of the public has exercised choice in selecting the transmissions, including the content of the transmissions or the time of receipt of such transmissions, or both, and as to which such member is charged a separate fee for each such transmission or specified group of transmissions;

'(B) from a copy of a transmission of a live event or an audiovisual work if such transmission is provided by a channel or service where payment is made by a member of the public for such channel or service in the form of a subscription fee that entitles the member of the public to receive all of the programming contained in such channel or service;

'(C) from a physical medium containing one or more prerecorded audiovisual works; or

'(D) from a copy of a transmission described in subparagraph (A) or from a copy made from a physical medium described in subparagraph (C).

In the event that a transmission meets both the conditions set forth in subparagraph (A) and those set forth in subparagraph (B), the transmission shall be treated as a transmission described in subparagraph (A).

'(3) INAPPLICABILITY- This subsection shall not—

'(A) require any analog video cassette camcorder to conform to the automatic gain control copy control technology with respect to any video signal received through a camera lens;

'(B) apply to the manufacture, importation, offer for sale, provision of, or other trafficking in, any professional analog video cassette recorder; or

'(C) apply to the offer for sale or provision of, or other trafficking in, any previously owned analog video cassette recorder, if such recorder was legally manufactured and sold when new and not subsequently modified in violation of paragraph (1)(B).

'(4) DEFINITIONS- For purposes of this subsection:

'(A) An 'analog video cassette recorder' means a device that records, or a device that includes a function that records, on electromagnetic tape in an analog format the electronic impulses produced by the video and audio portions of a television program, motion picture, or other form of audiovisual work.

'(B) An 'analog video cassette camcorder' means an analog video cassette recorder that contains a recording function that operates through a camera lens and through a video input that may be connected with a television or other video playback device.

'(C) An analog video cassette recorder 'conforms' to the automatic gain control copy control technology if it—

'(i) detects one or more of the elements of such technology and does not record the motion picture or transmission protected by such technology; or

'(ii) records a signal that, when played back, exhibits a meaningfully distorted or degraded display.

'(D) The term 'professional analog video cassette recorder' means an analog video cassette recorder that is designed, manufactured, marketed, and intended for use by a person who regularly employs such a device for a lawful business or industrial use, including making, performing, displaying, distributing, or transmitting copies of motion pictures on a commercial scale.

'(E) The terms 'VHS format', '8mm format', 'Beta format', 'automatic gain control copy control technology', 'colorstripe copy control technology', 'four-line version of the colorstripe copy control technology', and 'NTSC' have the meanings that are commonly understood in the consumer electronics and motion picture industries as of the date of the enactment of this chapter.

'(5) VIOLATIONS- Any violation of paragraph (1) of this subsection shall be treated as a violation of subsection (b)(1) of this section. Any violation of paragraph (2) of this subsection shall be deemed an 'act of circumvention' for the purposes of section 1203(c)(3)(A) of this chapter.

## 'Sec. 1202. Integrity of copyright management information

'(a) FALSE COPYRIGHT MANAGEMENT INFORMATION- No person shall knowingly and with the intent to induce, enable, facilitate, or conceal infringement—

'(1) provide copyright management information that is false, or

'(2) distribute or import for distribution copyright management information that is false.

'(b) REMOVAL OR ALTERATION OF COPYRIGHT MANAGEMENT INFORMATION- No person shall, without the authority of the copyright owner or the law—

'(1) intentionally remove or alter any copyright management information,

'(2) distribute or import for distribution copyright management information knowing that the copyright management information has been removed or altered without authority of the copyright owner or the law, or

'(3) distribute, import for distribution, or publicly perform works, copies of works, or phonorecords, knowing that copyright management information has been removed or altered without authority of the copyright owner or the law,

knowing, or, with respect to civil remedies under section 1203, having reasonable grounds to know, that it will induce, enable, facilitate, or conceal an infringement of any right under this title.

'(c) DEFINITION- As used in this section, the term 'copyright management information' means any of the following information conveyed in connection with copies or phonorecords of a work or performances or displays of a work, including in digital form, except that such term does not include any personally identifying information about a user of a work or of a copy, phonorecord, performance, or display of a work:

'(1) The title and other information identifying the work, including the information set forth on a notice of copyright.

'(2) The name of, and other identifying information about, the author of a work.

'(3) The name of, and other identifying information about, the copyright owner of the work, including the information set forth in a notice of copyright.

'(4) With the exception of public performances of works by radio and television broadcast stations, the name of, and other identifying information about, a performer whose performance is fixed in a work other than an audiovisual work.

'(5) With the exception of public performances of works by radio and television broadcast stations, in the case of an audiovisual work, the name of, and other identifying information about, a writer, performer, or director who is credited in the audiovisual work.

'(6) Terms and conditions for use of the work.

'(7) Identifying numbers or symbols referring to such information or links to such information.

'(8) Such other information as the Register of Copyrights may prescribe by regulation, except that the Register of Copyrights may not require the provision of any information concerning the user of a copyrighted work.

'(d) LAW ENFORCEMENT, INTELLIGENCE, AND OTHER GOVERNMENT ACTIVITIES- This section does not prohibit any lawfully authorized investigative, protective, information security, or intelligence activity of an officer, agent, or employee of the United States, a State, or a political subdivision of a State, or a person acting pursuant to a contract with the United States, a State, or a political subdivision of a State. For purposes of this subsection, the term 'information security' means activities carried out in order to identify and address the vulnerabilities of a government computer, computer system, or computer network.

'(e) LIMITATIONS ON LIABILITY-

'(1) ANALOG TRANSMISSIONS- In the case of an analog transmission, a person who is making transmissions in its capacity as a broadcast station, or as a cable system, or someone who provides programming to such station or system, shall not be liable for a violation of subsection (b) if—

'(A) avoiding the activity that constitutes such violation is not technically feasible or would create an undue financial hardship on such person; and

'(B) such person did not intend, by engaging in such activity, to induce, enable, facilitate, or conceal infringement of a right under this title.

'(2) DIGITAL TRANSMISSIONS-

'(A) If a digital transmission standard for the placement of copyright management information for a category of works is set in a voluntary, consensus standard-setting process involving a representative cross-section of broadcast stations or cable systems and copyright owners of a category of works that are intended for public performance by such stations or systems, a person identified in paragraph (1) shall not be liable for a violation of subsection (b) with respect to the particular copyright management information addressed by such standard if—

'(i) the placement of such information by someone other than such person is not in accordance with such standard; and

'(ii) the activity that constitutes such violation is not intended to induce, enable, facilitate, or conceal infringement of a right under this title.

'(B) Until a digital transmission standard has been set pursuant to subparagraph (A) with respect to the placement of copyright management information for a category or works, a person identified in paragraph (1) shall not be liable for a violation of subsection (b) with respect to such copyright management information, if the activity that constitutes such violation is not intended to induce, enable, facilitate, or conceal infringement of a right under this title, and if—

'(i) the transmission of such information by such person would result in a perceptible visual or aural degradation of the digital signal; or

'(ii) the transmission of such information by such person would conflict with—

'(I) an applicable government regulation relating to transmission of information in a digital signal;

'(II) an applicable industry-wide standard relating to the transmission of information in a digital signal that was adopted by a voluntary consensus standards body prior to the effective date of this chapter; or

'(III) an applicable industry-wide standard relating to the transmission of information in a digital signal that was adopted in a voluntary, consensus standards-setting process open to participation by a representative cross-section of broadcast stations or cable systems and copyright owners of a category of works that are intended for public performance by such stations or systems.

'(3) DEFINITIONS- As used in this subsection—

'(A) the term 'broadcast station' has the meaning given that term in section 3 of the Communications Act of 1934 (47 U.S.C. 153); and

'(B) the term 'cable system' has the meaning given that term in section 602 of the Communications Act of 1934 (47 U.S.C. 522).

## 'Sec. 1203. Civil remedies

'(a) CIVIL ACTIONS- Any person injured by a violation of section 1201 or 1202 may bring a civil action in an appropriate United States district court for such violation.

'(b) POWERS OF THE COURT- In an action brought under subsection (a), the court—

'(1) may grant temporary and permanent injunctions on such terms as it deems reasonable to prevent or restrain a violation, but in no event shall impose a prior restraint on free speech or the press protected under the 1st amendment to the Constitution;

'(2) at any time while an action is pending, may order the impounding, on such terms as it deems reasonable, of any device or product that is in the custody or control of the alleged violator and that the court has reasonable cause to believe was involved in a violation;

'(3) may award damages under subsection (c);

'(4) in its discretion may allow the recovery of costs by or against any party other than the United States or an officer thereof;

'(5) in its discretion may award reasonable attorney's fees to the prevailing party; and

'(6) may, as part of a final judgment or decree finding a violation, order the remedial modification or the destruction of any device or product involved in the violation that is in the custody or control of the violator or has been impounded under paragraph (2).

'(c) AWARD OF DAMAGES-

'(1) IN GENERAL- Except as otherwise provided in this title, a person committing a violation of section 1201 or 1202 is liable for either—

'(A) the actual damages and any additional profits of the violator, as provided in paragraph (2), or

'(B) statutory damages, as provided in paragraph (3).

'(2) ACTUAL DAMAGES- The court shall award to the complaining party the actual damages suffered by the party as a result of the violation, and any profits of the violator that are attributable to the violation and are not taken into account in computing the actual damages, if the complaining party elects such damages at any time before final judgment is entered.

'(3) STATUTORY DAMAGES- (A) At any time before final judgment is entered, a complaining party may elect to recover an award of statutory damages for each violation of section 1201 in the sum of not less than $200 or more than $2,500 per act of circumvention, device, product, component, offer, or performance of service, as the court considers just.

'(B) At any time before final judgment is entered, a complaining party may elect to recover an award of statutory damages for each violation of section 1202 in the sum of not less than $2,500 or more than $25,000.

'(4) REPEATED VIOLATIONS- In any case in which the injured party sustains the burden of proving, and the court finds, that a person has violated section 1201 or 1202 within 3 years after a final judgment was entered against the person for another such violation, the court may increase the award of damages up to triple the amount that would otherwise be awarded, as the court considers just.

'(5) Innocent violations-

'(A) IN GENERAL- The court in its discretion may reduce or remit the total award of damages in any case in which the violator sustains the burden of proving, and the court finds, that the violator was not aware and had no reason to believe that its acts constituted a violation.

'(B) NONPROFIT LIBRARY, ARCHIVES, OR EDUCA-TIONAL INSTITUTIONS- In the case of a nonprofit library, archives, or educational institution, the court shall remit damages in any case in which the library, archives, or educational institution sustains the burden of proving, and the court finds, that the library, archives, or educational institution was not aware and had no reason to believe that its acts constituted a violation.

### 'Sec. 1204. Criminal offenses and penalties

'(a) IN GENERAL- Any person who violates section 1201 or 1202 willfully and for purposes of commercial advantage or private financial gain—

'(1) shall be fined not more than $500,000 or imprisoned for not more than 5 years, or both, for the first offense; and

'(2) shall be fined not more than $1,000,000 or imprisoned for not more than 10 years, or both, for any subsequent offense.

'(b) LIMITATION FOR NONPROFIT LIBRARY, ARCHIVES, OR EDUCATIONAL INSTITUTION- Subsection (a) shall not apply to a nonprofit library, archives, or educational institution.

'(c) STATUTE OF LIMITATIONS- No criminal proceeding shall be brought under this section unless such proceeding is commenced within 5 years after the cause of action arose.

### 'Sec. 1205. Savings clause

'Nothing in this chapter abrogates, diminishes, or weakens the provisions of, nor provides any defense or element of mitigation in a criminal prosecution or civil action under, any Federal or State law that prevents the violation of the privacy of an individual in connection with the individual's use of the Internet.'.

(b) CONFORMING AMENDMENT- The table of chapters for title 17, United States Code, is amended by adding after the item relating to chapter 11 the following:

1201'.

## SEC. 104. EVALUATION OF IMPACT OF COPYRIGHT LAW AND AMENDMENTS ON ELECTRONIC COMMERCE AND TECHNOLOGICAL DEVELOPMENT.

(a) EVALUATION BY THE REGISTER OF COPYRIGHTS AND THE ASSISTANT SECRETARY FOR COMMUNICATIONS AND INFORMATION- The Register of Copyrights and the Assistant Secretary for Communications and Information of the Department of Commerce shall jointly evaluate—

(1) the effects of the amendments made by this title and the development of electronic commerce and associated technology on the operation of sections 109 and 117 of title 17, United States Code; and

(2) the relationship between existing and emergent technology and the operation of sections 109 and 117 of title 17, United States Code.

(b) REPORT TO CONGRESS- The Register of Copyrights and the Assistant Secretary for Communications and Information of the Department of Commerce shall, not later than 24 months after the date of the enactment of this Act, submit to the Congress a joint report on the evaluation conducted under subsection (a), including any legislative recommendations the Register and the Assistant Secretary may have.

## SEC. 105. EFFECTIVE DATE.

(a) IN GENERAL- Except as otherwise provided in this title, this title and the amendments made by this title shall take effect on the date of the enactment of this Act.

(b) AMENDMENTS RELATING TO CERTAIN INTERNA-
TIONAL AGREEMENTS- (1) The following shall take effect upon
the entry into force of the WIPO Copyright Treaty with respect to
the United States:

(A) Paragraph (5) of the definition of 'international agreement'
contained in section 101 of title 17, United States Code, as
amended by section 102(a)(4) of this Act.

(B) The amendment made by section 102(a)(6) of this Act.

(C) Subparagraph (C) of section 104A(h)(1) of title 17, United
States Code, as amended by section 102(c)(1) of this Act.

(D) Subparagraph (C) of section 104A(h)(3) of title 17, United
States Code, as amended by section 102(c)(2) of this Act.

(2) The following shall take effect upon the entry into force of the
WIPO Performances and Phonograms Treaty with respect to the
United States:

(A) Paragraph (6) of the definition of 'international agreement'
contained in section 101 of title 17, United States Code, as
amended by section 102(a)(4) of this Act.

(B) The amendment made by section 102(a)(7) of this Act.

(C) The amendment made by section 102(b)(2) of this Act.

(D) Subparagraph (D) of section 104A(h)(1) of title 17, United
States Code, as amended by section 102(c)(1) of this Act.

(E) Subparagraph (D) of section 104A(h)(3) of title 17, United
States Code, as amended by section 102(c)(2) of this Act.

(F) The amendments made by section 102(c)(3) of this Act.

## TITLE II—ONLINE COPYRIGHT INFRINGEMENT LIABILITY LIMITATION

### SEC. 201. SHORT TITLE.

This title may be cited as the 'Online Copyright Infringement Liability Limitation Act'.

### SEC. 202. LIMITATIONS ON LIABILITY FOR COPYRIGHT INFRINGEMENT.

(a) IN GENERAL- Chapter 5 of title 17, United States Code, is amended by adding after section 511 the following new section:

**'Sec. 512. Limitations on liability relating to material online**

'(a) TRANSITORY DIGITAL NETWORK COMMUNICATIONS- A service provider shall not be liable for monetary relief, or, except as provided in subsection (j), for injunctive or other equitable relief, for infringement of copyright by reason of the provider's transmitting, routing, or providing connections for, material through a system or network controlled or operated by or for the service provider, or by reason of the intermediate and transient storage of that material in the course of such transmitting, routing, or providing connections, if—

'(1) the transmission of the material was initiated by or at the direction of a person other than the service provider;

'(2) the transmission, routing, provision of connections, or storage is carried out through an automatic technical process without selection of the material by the service provider;

'(3) the service provider does not select the recipients of the material except as an automatic response to the request of another person;

'(4) no copy of the material made by the service provider in the course of such intermediate or transient storage is maintained on the system or network in a manner ordinarily accessible to anyone other than anticipated recipients, and no such copy is maintained on the system or network in a manner ordinarily accessible to such anticipated recipients for a longer period than is reasonably necessary for the transmission, routing, or provision of connections; and

'(5) the material is transmitted through the system or network without modification of its content.

'(b) SYSTEM CACHING-

'(1) LIMITATION ON LIABILITY- A service provider shall not be liable for monetary relief, or, except as provided in subsection (j), for injunctive or other equitable relief, for infringement of copyright by reason of the intermediate and temporary storage of material on a system or network controlled or operated by or for the service provider in a case in which—

'(A) the material is made available online by a person other than the service provider;

'(B) the material is transmitted from the person described in subparagraph (A) through the system or network to a person other than the person described in subparagraph (A) at the direction of that other person; and

'(C) the storage is carried out through an automatic technical process for the purpose of making the material available to users of the system or network who, after the material is transmitted as described in subparagraph (B), request access to the material from the person described in subparagraph (A),

if the conditions set forth in paragraph (2) are met.

(2) CONDITIONS- The conditions referred to in paragraph (1) are that—

'(A) the material described in paragraph (1) is transmitted to the subsequent users described in paragraph (1)(C) without modification to its content from the manner in which the material was transmitted from the person described in paragraph (1)(A);

'(B) the service provider described in paragraph (1) complies with rules concerning the refreshing, reloading, or other updating of the material when specified by the person making the material available online in accordance with a generally accepted industry standard data communications protocol for the system or network through which that person makes the material available, except that this subparagraph applies only if those rules are not used by the person described in paragraph (1)(A) to prevent or unreasonably impair the intermediate storage to which this subsection applies;

'(C) the service provider does not interfere with the ability of technology associated with the material to return to the person described in paragraph (1)(A) the information that would have been available to that person if the material had been obtained by the subsequent users described in paragraph (1)(C) directly from that person, except that this subparagraph applies only if that technology—

> '(i) does not significantly interfere with the performance of the provider's system or network or with the intermediate storage of the material;

> '(ii) is consistent with generally accepted industry standard communications protocols; and

> '(iii) does not extract information from the provider's system or network other than the information that would have been available to the person described in paragraph (1)(A) if the subsequent users had gained access to the material directly from that person;

'(D) if the person described in paragraph (1)(A) has in effect a condition that a person must meet prior to having access to the material, such as a condition based on payment of a fee or provision of a password or other information, the service provider permits access to the stored material in significant part only to users of its system or network that have met those conditions and only in accordance with those conditions; and

'(E) if the person described in paragraph (1)(A) makes that material available online without the authorization of the copyright owner of the material, the service provider responds expeditiously to remove, or disable access to, the material that is claimed to be infringing upon notification of claimed infringement as described in subsection (c)(3), except that this subparagraph applies only if—

'(i) the material has previously been removed from the originating site or access to it has been disabled, or a court has ordered that the material be removed from the originating site or that access to the material on the originating site be disabled; and

'(ii) the party giving the notification includes in the notification a statement confirming that the material has been removed from the originating site or access to it has been disabled or that a court has ordered that the material be removed from the originating site or that access to the material on the originating site be disabled.

'(c) INFORMATION RESIDING ON SYSTEMS OR NETWORKS AT DIRECTION OF USERS-

'(1) IN GENERAL- A service provider shall not be liable for monetary relief, or, except as provided in subsection (j), for injunctive or other equitable relief, for infringement of copyright by reason of the storage at the direction of a user of material that resides on a system or network controlled or operated by or for the service provider, if the service provider—

'(A)(i) does not have actual knowledge that the material or an activity using the material on the system or network is infringing;

'(ii) in the absence of such actual knowledge, is not aware of facts or circumstances from which infringing activity is apparent; or

'(iii) upon obtaining such knowledge or awareness, acts expeditiously to remove, or disable access to, the material;

'(B) does not receive a financial benefit directly attributable to the infringing activity, in a case in which the service provider has the right and ability to control such activity; and

'(C) upon notification of claimed infringement as described in paragraph (3), responds expeditiously to remove, or disable access to, the material that is claimed to be infringing or to be the subject of infringing activity.

'(2) DESIGNATED AGENT- The limitations on liability established in this subsection apply to a service provider only if the service provider has designated an agent to receive notifications of claimed infringement described in paragraph (3), by making available through its service, including on its website in a location accessible to the public, and by providing to the Copyright Office, substantially the following information:

'(A) the name, address, phone number, and electronic mail address of the agent.

'(B) other contact information which the Register of Copyrights may deem appropriate.

The Register of Copyrights shall maintain a current directory of agents available to the public for inspection, including through the Internet, in both electronic and hard copy formats, and may require payment of a fee by service providers to cover the costs of maintaining the directory.

'(3) ELEMENTS OF NOTIFICATION-

'(A) To be effective under this subsection, a notification of claimed infringement must be a written communication provided to the designated agent of a service provider that includes substantially the following:

'(i) A physical or electronic signature of a person authorized to act on behalf of the owner of an exclusive right that is allegedly infringed.

'(ii) Identification of the copyrighted work claimed to have been infringed, or, if multiple copyrighted works at a single online site are covered by a single notification, a representative list of such works at that site.

'(iii) Identification of the material that is claimed to be infringing or to be the subject of infringing activity and that is to be removed or access to which is to be disabled, and information reasonably sufficient to permit the service provider to locate the material.

'(iv) Information reasonably sufficient to permit the service provider to contact the complaining party, such as an address, telephone number, and, if available, an electronic mail address at which the complaining party may be contacted.

'(v) A statement that the complaining party has a good faith belief that use of the material in the manner complained of is not authorized by the copyright owner, its agent, or the law.

'(vi) A statement that the information in the notification is accurate, and under penalty of perjury, that the complaining party is authorized to act on behalf of the owner of an exclusive right that is allegedly infringed.

'(B)(i) Subject to clause (ii), a notification from a copyright owner or from a person authorized to act on behalf of the copyright owner that fails to comply substantially with the provisions of subparagraph (A) shall not be considered under paragraph (1)(A) in determining whether a service provider has actual knowledge or is aware of facts or circumstances from which infringing activity is apparent.

'(ii) In a case in which the notification that is provided to the service provider's designated agent fails to comply substantially with all the provisions of subparagraph (A) but substantially complies with clauses (ii), (iii), and (iv) of subparagraph (A), clause (i) of this subparagraph applies only if the service provider promptly attempts to contact the person making the notification or takes other reasonable steps to assist in the receipt of notification that substantially complies with all the provisions of subparagraph (A).

'(d) INFORMATION LOCATION TOOLS- A service provider shall not be liable for monetary relief, or, except as provided in subsection (j), for injunctive or other equitable relief, for infringement of copyright by reason of the provider referring or linking users to an online location containing infringing material or infringing activity, by using information location tools, including a directory, index, reference, pointer, or hypertext link, if the service provider—

'(1)(A) does not have actual knowledge that the material or activity is infringing;

'(B) in the absence of such actual knowledge, is not aware of facts or circumstances from which infringing activity is apparent; or

'(C) upon obtaining such knowledge or awareness, acts expeditiously to remove, or disable access to, the material;

'(2) does not receive a financial benefit directly attributable to the infringing activity, in a case in which the service provider has the right and ability to control such activity; and

'(3) upon notification of claimed infringement as described in subsection (c)(3), responds expeditiously to remove, or disable access to, the material that is claimed to be infringing or to be the subject of infringing activity, except that, for purposes of this paragraph, the information described in subsection (c)(3)(A)(iii) shall be identification of the reference or link, to material or activity claimed to be infringing, that is to be removed or access to which is to be disabled, and information reasonably sufficient to permit the service provider to locate that reference or link.

'(e) LIMITATION ON LIABILITY OF NONPROFIT EDUCATIONAL INSTITUTIONS- (1) When a public or other nonprofit institution of higher education is a service provider, and when a faculty member or graduate student who is an employee of such institution is performing a teaching or research function, for the purposes of subsections (a) and (b) such faculty member or graduate student shall be considered to be a person other than the institution, and for the purposes of subsections (c) and (d) such faculty member's or graduate student's knowledge or awareness of his or her infringing activities shall not be attributed to the institution, if—

'(A) such faculty member's or graduate student's infringing activities do not involve the provision of online access to instructional materials that are or were required or recommended, within the preceding 3-year period, for a course taught at the institution by such faculty member or graduate student;

'(B) the institution has not, within the preceding 3-year period, received more than two notifications described in subsection (c)(3) of claimed infringement by such faculty member or graduate student, and such notifications of claimed infringement were not actionable under subsection (f); and

'(C) the institution provides to all users of its system or network informational materials that accurately describe, and promote compliance with, the laws of the United States relating to copyright.

'(2) INJUNCTIONS- For the purposes of this subsection, the limitations on injunctive relief contained in subsections (j)(2) and (j)(3), but not those in (j)(1), shall apply.

'(f) MISREPRESENTATIONS- Any person who knowingly materially misrepresents under this section—

'(1) that material or activity is infringing, or

'(2) that material or activity was removed or disabled by mistake or misidentification, shall be liable for any damages, including costs and attorneys' fees, incurred by the alleged infringer, by any copyright owner or copyright owner's authorized licensee, or by a service provider, who is injured by such misrepresentation, as the result of the service provider relying upon such misrepresentation in removing or disabling access to the material or activity claimed to be infringing, or in replacing the removed material or ceasing to disable access to it.

'(g) REPLACEMENT OF REMOVED OR DISABLED MATERIAL AND LIMITATION ON OTHER LIABILITY-

'(1) NO LIABILITY FOR TAKING DOWN GENERALLY- Subject to paragraph (2), a service provider shall not be liable to any person for any claim based on the service provider's good faith disabling of access to, or removal of, material or activity claimed to be infringing or based on facts or circumstances from which infringing activity is apparent, regardless of whether the material or activity is ultimately determined to be infringing.

'(2) EXCEPTION- Paragraph (1) shall not apply with respect to material residing at the direction of a subscriber of the service provider on a system or network controlled or operated by or for the service provider that is removed, or to which access is disabled by the service provider, pursuant to a notice provided under subsection (c)(1)(C), unless the service provider—

'(A) takes reasonable steps promptly to notify the subscriber that it has removed or disabled access to the material;

'(B) upon receipt of a counter notification described in paragraph (3), promptly provides the person who provided the notification under subsection (c)(1)(C) with a copy of the counter notification, and informs that person that it will replace the removed material or cease disabling access to it in 10 business days; and

'(C) replaces the removed material and ceases disabling access to it not less than 10, nor more than 14, business days following receipt of the counter notice, unless its designated agent first receives notice from the person who submitted the notification under subsection (c)(1)(C) that such person has filed an action seeking a court order to restrain the subscriber from engaging in infringing activity relating to the material on the service provider's system or network.

'(3) CONTENTS OF COUNTER NOTIFICATION- To be effective under this subsection, a counter notification must be a written communication provided to the service provider's designated agent that includes substantially the following:

'(A) A physical or electronic signature of the subscriber.

'(B) Identification of the material that has been removed or to which access has been disabled and the location at which the material appeared before it was removed or access to it was disabled.

'(C) A statement under penalty of perjury that the subscriber has a good faith belief that the material was removed or disabled as a result of mistake or misidentification of the material to be removed or disabled.

'(D) The subscriber's name, address, and telephone number, and a statement that the subscriber consents to the jurisdiction of Federal District Court for the judicial district in which the address is located, or if the subscriber's address is outside of the United States, for any judicial district in which the service provider may be found, and that the subscriber will accept service of process from the person who provided notification under subsection (c)(1)(C) or an agent of such person.

'(4) LIMITATION ON OTHER LIABILITY- A service provider's compliance with paragraph (2) shall not subject the service provider to liability for copyright infringement with respect to the material identified in the notice provided under subsection (c)(1)(C).

'(h) SUBPOENA TO IDENTIFY INFRINGER-

'(1) REQUEST- A copyright owner or a person authorized to act on the owner's behalf may request the clerk of any United States district court to issue a subpoena to a service provider for identification of an alleged infringer in accordance with this subsection.

'(2) CONTENTS OF REQUEST- The request may be made by filing with the clerk—

'(A) a copy of a notification described in subsection (c)(3)(A);

'(B) a proposed subpoena; and

'(C) a sworn declaration to the effect that the purpose for which the subpoena is sought is to obtain the identity of an alleged infringer and that such information will only be used for the purpose of protecting rights under this title.

'(3) CONTENTS OF SUBPOENA- The subpoena shall authorize and order the service provider receiving the notification and the subpoena to expeditiously disclose to the copyright owner or person authorized by the copyright owner information sufficient to identify the alleged infringer of the material described in the notification to the extent such information is available to the service provider.

'(4) BASIS FOR GRANTING SUBPOENA- If the notification filed satisfies the provisions of subsection (c)(3)(A), the proposed subpoena is in proper form, and the accompanying declaration is properly executed, the clerk shall expeditiously issue and sign the proposed subpoena and return it to the requester for delivery to the service provider.

'(5) ACTIONS OF SERVICE PROVIDER RECEIVING SUBPOENA- Upon receipt of the issued subpoena, either accompanying or subsequent to the receipt of a notification described in subsection (c)(3)(A), the service provider shall expeditiously disclose to the copyright owner or person authorized by the copyright owner the information required by the subpoena, notwithstanding any other provision of law and regardless of whether the service provider responds to the notification.

'(6) RULES APPLICABLE TO SUBPOENA- Unless otherwise provided by this section or by applicable rules of the court, the procedure for issuance and delivery of the subpoena, and the remedies for noncompliance with the subpoena, shall be governed to the greatest extent practicable by those provisions of the Federal Rules of Civil Procedure governing the issuance, service, and enforcement of a subpoena duces tecum.

'(i) CONDITIONS FOR ELIGIBILITY-

'(1) ACCOMMODATION OF TECHNOLOGY- The limitations on liability established by this section shall apply to a service provider only if the service provider—

'(A) has adopted and reasonably implemented, and informs subscribers and account holders of the service provider's system or network of, a policy that provides for the termination in appropriate circumstances of subscribers and account holders of the service provider's system or network who are repeat infringers; and

'(B) accommodates and does not interfere with standard technical measures.

'(2) DEFINITION- As used in this subsection, the term 'standard technical measures' means technical measures that are used by copyright owners to identify or protect copyrighted works and—

'(A) have been developed pursuant to a broad consensus of copyright owners and service providers in an open, fair, voluntary, multi-industry standards process;

'(B) are available to any person on reasonable and nondiscriminatory terms; and

'(C) do not impose substantial costs on service providers or substantial burdens on their systems or networks.

'(j) INJUNCTIONS- The following rules shall apply in the case of any application for an injunction under section 502 against a service provider that is not subject to monetary remedies under this section:

'(1) SCOPE OF RELIEF- (A) With respect to conduct other than that which qualifies for the limitation on remedies set forth in subsection (a), the court may grant injunctive relief with respect to a service provider only in one or more of the following forms:

'(i) An order restraining the service provider from providing access to infringing material or activity residing at a particular online site on the provider's system or network.

'(ii) An order restraining the service provider from providing access to a subscriber or account holder of the service provider's system or network who is engaging in infringing activity and is identified in the order, by terminating the accounts of the subscriber or account holder that are specified in the order.

'(iii) Such other injunctive relief as the court may consider necessary to prevent or restrain infringement of copyrighted material specified in the order of the court at a particular online location, if such relief is the least burdensome to the service provider among the forms of relief comparably effective for that purpose.

'(B) If the service provider qualifies for the limitation on remedies described in subsection (a), the court may only grant injunctive relief in one or both of the following forms:

'(i) An order restraining the service provider from providing access to a subscriber or account holder of the service provider's system or network who is using the provider's service to engage in infringing activity and is identified in the order, by terminating the accounts of the subscriber or account holder that are specified in the order.

'(ii) An order restraining the service provider from providing access, by taking reasonable steps specified in the order to block access, to a specific, identified, online location outside the United States.

'(2) CONSIDERATIONS- The court, in considering the relevant criteria for injunctive relief under applicable law, shall consider—

'(A) whether such an injunction, either alone or in combination with other such injunctions issued against the same service provider under this subsection, would significantly burden either the provider or the operation of the provider's system or network;

'(B) the magnitude of the harm likely to be suffered by the copyright owner in the digital network environment if steps are not taken to prevent or restrain the infringement;

'(C) whether implementation of such an injunction would be technically feasible and effective, and would not interfere with access to noninfringing material at other online locations; and

'(D) whether other less burdensome and comparably effective means of preventing or restraining access to the infringing material are available.

'(3) NOTICE AND EX PARTE ORDERS- Injunctive relief under this subsection shall be available only after notice to the service provider and an opportunity for the service provider to appear are provided, except for orders ensuring the preservation of evidence or other orders having no material adverse effect on the operation of the service provider's communications network.

'(k) DEFINITIONS-

'(1) SERVICE PROVIDER- (A) As used in subsection (a), the term 'service provider' means an entity offering the transmission, routing, or providing of connections for digital online communications, between or among points specified by a user, of material of the user's choosing, without modification to the content of the material as sent or received.

'(B) As used in this section, other than subsection (a), the term 'service provider' means a provider of online services or network access, or the operator of facilities therefor, and includes an entity described in subparagraph (A).

'(2) MONETARY RELIEF- As used in this section, the term 'monetary relief' means damages, costs, attorneys' fees, and any other form of monetary payment.

'(l) OTHER DEFENSES NOT AFFECTED- The failure of a service provider's conduct to qualify for limitation of liability under this section shall not bear adversely upon the consideration of a defense by the service provider that the service provider's conduct is not infringing under this title or any other defense.

'(m) PROTECTION OF PRIVACY- Nothing in this section shall be construed to condition the applicability of subsections (a) through (d) on—

'(1) a service provider monitoring its service or affirmatively seeking facts indicating infringing activity, except to the extent consistent with a standard technical measure complying with the provisions of subsection (i); or

'(2) a service provider gaining access to, removing, or disabling access to material in cases in which such conduct is prohibited by law.

'(n) CONSTRUCTION- Subsections (a), (b), (c), and (d) describe separate and distinct functions for purposes of applying this section. Whether a service provider qualifies for the limitation on liability in any one of those subsections shall be based solely on the criteria in that subsection, and shall not affect a determination of whether that service provider qualifies for the limitations on liability under any other such subsection.'.

(b) CONFORMING AMENDMENT- The table of sections for chapter 5 of title 17, United States Code, is amended by adding at the end the following:

'512. Limitations on liability relating to material online.'.

## SEC. 203. EFFECTIVE DATE.

This title and the amendments made by this title shall take effect on the date of the enactment of this Act.

### TITLE III—COMPUTER MAINTENANCE OR REPAIR COPYRIGHT EXEMPTION

## SEC. 301. SHORT TITLE.

This title may be cited as the 'Computer Maintenance Competition Assurance Act'.

## SEC. 302. LIMITATIONS ON EXCLUSIVE RIGHTS; COMPUTER PROGRAMS.

Section 117 of title 17, United States Code, is amended—

(1) by striking 'Notwithstanding' and inserting the following:

'(a) MAKING OF ADDITIONAL COPY OR ADAPTATION BY OWNER OF COPY- Notwithstanding';

(2) by striking 'Any exact' and inserting the following:

'(b) LEASE, SALE, OR OTHER TRANSFER OF ADDITIONAL COPY OR ADAPTATION- Any exact'; and

(3) by adding at the end the following:

'(c) MACHINE MAINTENANCE OR REPAIR- Notwithstanding the provisions of section 106, it is not an infringement for the owner or lessee of a machine to make or authorize the making of a copy of a computer program if such copy is made solely by virtue of the activation of a machine that lawfully contains an authorized copy of the computer program, for purposes only of maintenance or repair of that machine, if—

'(1) such new copy is used in no other manner and is destroyed immediately after the maintenance or repair is completed; and

'(2) with respect to any computer program or part thereof that is not necessary for that machine to be activated, such program or part thereof is not accessed or used other than to make such new copy by virtue of the activation of the machine.

'(d) DEFINITIONS- For purposes of this section—

'(1) the 'maintenance' of a machine is the servicing of the machine in order to make it work in accordance with its original specifications and any changes to those specifications authorized for that machine; and

'(2) the 'repair' of a machine is the restoring of the machine to the state of working in accordance with its original specifications and any changes to those specifications authorized for that machine.'.

## TITLE IV—MISCELLANEOUS PROVISIONS

## SEC. 401. PROVISIONS RELATING TO THE COMMISSIONER OF PATENTS AND TRADEMARKS AND THE REGISTER OF COPYRIGHTS

(a) COMPENSATION- (1) Section 3(d) of title 35, United States Code, is amended by striking 'prescribed by law for Assistant Secretaries of Commerce' and inserting 'in effect for level III of the

Executive Schedule under section 5314 of title 5, United States Code'.

(2) Section 701(e) of title 17, United States Code, is amended—

(A) by striking 'IV' and inserting 'III'; and

(B) by striking '5315' and inserting '5314'.

(3) Section 5314 of title 5, United States Code, is amended by adding at the end the following:

'Assistant Secretary of Commerce and Commissioner of Patents and Trademarks.

'Register of Copyrights.'.

(b) CLARIFICATION OF AUTHORITY OF THE COPY-RIGHT OFFICE- Section 701 of title 17, United States Code, is amended—

(1) by redesignating subsections (b) through (e) as subsections (c) through (f), respectively; and

(2) by inserting after subsection (a) the following:

'(b) In addition to the functions and duties set out elsewhere in this chapter, the Register of Copyrights shall perform the following functions:

'(1) Advise Congress on national and international issues relating to copyright, other matters arising under this title, and related matters.

'(2) Provide information and assistance to Federal departments and agencies and the Judiciary on national and international issues relating to copyright, other matters arising under this title, and related matters.

'(3) Participate in meetings of international intergovernmental organizations and meetings with foreign government officials relating to copyright, other matters arising under this title, and related matters, including as a member of United States delegations as authorized by the appropriate Executive branch authority.

'(4) Conduct studies and programs regarding copyright, other matters arising under this title, and related matters, the administration of the Copyright Office, or any function vested in the Copyright Office by law, including educational programs conducted cooperatively with foreign intellectual property offices and international intergovernmental organizations.

'(5) Perform such other functions as Congress may direct, or as may be appropriate in furtherance of the functions and duties specifically set forth in this title.'.

## SEC. 402. EPHEMERAL RECORDINGS.

Section 112(a) of title 17, United States Code, is amended—

(1) by redesignating paragraphs (1), (2), and (3) as subparagraphs (A), (B), and (C), respectively;

(2) by inserting '(1)' after '(a)';

(3) by inserting after 'under a license' the following: ', including a statutory license under section 114(f),';

(4) by inserting after '114(a),' the following: 'or for a transmitting organization that is a broadcast radio or television station licensed as such by the Federal Communications Commission and that makes a broadcast transmission of a performance of a sound recording in a digital format on a nonsubscription basis,'; and

(5) by adding at the end the following:

'(2) In a case in which a transmitting organization entitled to make a copy or phonorecord under paragraph (1) in connection with the transmission to the public of a performance or display of a work is prevented from making such copy or phonorecord by reason of the application by the copyright owner of technical measures that prevent the reproduction of the work, the copyright owner shall make available to the transmitting organization the necessary means for permitting the making of such copy or phonorecord as permitted under that paragraph, if it is technologically feasible and economically reasonable for the copyright owner to do so. If the copyright owner fails to do so in a timely manner in light of the transmitting organization's reasonable business requirements, the transmitting organization shall not be liable for a violation of section 1201(a)(1) of this title for engaging in such activities as are necessary to make such copies or phonorecords as permitted under paragraph (1) of this subsection.'.

## SEC. 403. LIMITATIONS ON EXCLUSIVE RIGHTS; DISTANCE EDUCATION.

(a) RECOMMENDATIONS BY REGISTER OF COPY-RIGHTS- Not later than 6 months after the date of the enactment of this Act, the Register of Copyrights, after consultation with representatives of copyright owners, nonprofit educational institutions, and nonprofit libraries and archives, shall submit to the Congress recommendations on how to promote distance education through digital technologies, including interactive digital networks, while maintaining an appropriate balance between the rights of copyright owners and the needs of users of copyrighted works. Such recommendations shall include any legislation the Register of Copyrights considers appropriate to achieve the objective described in the preceding sentence.

(b) FACTORS- In formulating recommendations under subsection (a), the Register of Copyrights shall consider—

(1) the need for an exemption from exclusive rights of copyright owners for distance education through digital networks;

(2) the categories of works to be included under any distance education exemption;

(3) the extent of appropriate quantitative limitations on the portions of works that may be used under any distance education exemption;

(4) the parties who should be entitled to the benefits of any distance education exemption;

(5) the parties who should be designated as eligible recipients of distance education materials under any distance education exemption;

(6) whether and what types of technological measures can or should be employed to safeguard against unauthorized access to, and use or retention of, copyrighted materials as a condition of eligibility for any distance education exemption, including,

in light of developing technological capabilities, the exemption set out in section 110(2) of title 17, United States Code;

(7) the extent to which the availability of licenses for the use of copyrighted works in distance education through interactive digital networks should be considered in assessing eligibility for any distance education exemption; and

(8) such other issues relating to distance education through interactive digital networks that the Register considers appropriate.

## SEC. 404. EXEMPTION FOR LIBRARIES AND ARCHIVES.

Section 108 of title 17, United States Code, is amended—

(1) in subsection (a)—

(A) by striking 'Notwithstanding' and inserting 'Except as otherwise provided in this title and notwithstanding';

(B) by inserting after 'no more than one copy or phonorecord of a work' the following: ', except as provided in subsections (b) and (c)'; and

(C) in paragraph (3) by inserting after 'copyright' the following: 'that appears on the copy or phonorecord that is reproduced under the provisions of this section, or includes a legend stating that the work may be protected by copyright if no such notice can be found on the copy or phonorecord that is reproduced under the provisions of this section';

(2) in subsection (b)—

(A) by striking 'a copy or phonorecord' and inserting 'three copies or phonorecords';

(B) by striking 'in facsimile form'; and

(C) by striking 'if the copy or phonorecord reproduced is currently in the collections of the library or archives.' and inserting 'if—

'(1) the copy or phonorecord reproduced is currently in the collections of the library or archives; and

'(2) any such copy or phonorecord that is reproduced in digital format is not otherwise distributed in that format and is not made available to the public in that format outside the premises of the library or archives.'; and

(3) in subsection (c)—

(A) by striking 'a copy or phonorecord' and inserting 'three copies or phonorecords';

(B) by striking 'in facsimile form';

(C) by inserting 'or if the existing format in which the work is stored has become obsolete,' after 'stolen,';

(D) by striking 'if the library or archives has, after a reasonable effort, determined that an unused replacement cannot be obtained at a fair price.' and inserting 'if—

'(1) the library or archives has, after a reasonable effort, determined that an unused replacement cannot be obtained at a fair price; and

'(2) any such copy or phonorecord that is reproduced in digital format is not made available to the public in that format outside the premises of the library or archives in lawful possession of such copy.'; and

(E) by adding at the end the following:

'For purposes of this subsection, a format shall be considered obsolete if the machine or device necessary to render perceptible a work stored in that format is no longer manufactured or is no longer reasonably available in the commercial marketplace.'.

## SEC. 405. SCOPE OF EXCLUSIVE RIGHTS IN SOUND RECORDINGS; EPHEMERAL RECORDINGS.

(a) SCOPE OF EXCLUSIVE RIGHTS IN SOUND RECORD-INGS- Section 114 of title 17, United States Code, is amended as follows:

(1) Subsection (d) is amended—

(A) in paragraph (1) by striking subparagraph (A) and inserting the following:

'(A) a nonsubscription broadcast transmission;'; and

(B) by amending paragraph (2) to read as follows:

'(2) STATUTORY LICENSING OF CERTAIN TRANS-MISSIONS- The performance of a sound recording publicly by means of a subscription digital audio transmission not exempt under paragraph (1), an eligible nonsubscription transmission, or a transmission not exempt under paragraph (1) that is made by a preexisting satellite digital audio radio service shall be subject to statutory licensing, in accordance with subsection (f) if—

'(A)(i) the transmission is not part of an interactive service;

'(ii) except in the case of a transmission to a business establishment, the transmitting entity does not automatically and intentionally cause any device receiving the transmission to switch from one program channel to another; and

'(iii) except as provided in section 1002(e), the transmission of the sound recording is accompanied, if technically feasible, by the information encoded in that sound recording, if any, by or under the authority of the copyright owner of that sound recording, that identifies the title of the sound recording, the featured recording artist who performs on the sound recording, and related information, including information concerning the underlying musical work and its writer;

'(B) in the case of a subscription transmission not exempt under paragraph (1) that is made by a preexisting subscription service in the same transmission medium used by such service on July 31, 1998, or in the case of a transmission not exempt under paragraph (1) that is made by a preexisting satellite digital audio radio service—

'(i) the transmission does not exceed the sound recording performance complement; and

'(ii) the transmitting entity does not cause to be published by means of an advance program schedule or prior announcement the titles of the specific sound recordings or phonorecords embodying such sound recordings to be transmitted; and

'(C) in the case of an eligible nonsubscription transmission or a subscription transmission not exempt under paragraph (1) that is made by a new subscription service or by a preexisting subscription service other than in the same transmission medium used by such service on July 31, 1998—

'(i) the transmission does not exceed the sound recording performance complement, except that this requirement shall not apply in the case of a retransmission of a broadcast transmission if the retransmission is made by a transmitting entity that does not have the right or ability to control the programming of the broadcast station making the broadcast transmission, unless—

'(I) the broadcast station makes broadcast transmissions—

'(aa) in digital format that regularly exceed the sound recording performance complement; or '(bb) in analog format, a substantial portion of which, on a weekly basis, exceed the sound recording performance complement; and

'(II) the sound recording copyright owner or its representative has notified the transmitting entity in writing that broadcast transmissions of the copyright owner's sound recordings exceed the sound recording performance complement as provided in this clause;

'(ii) the transmitting entity does not cause to be published, or induce or facilitate the publication, by means of an advance program schedule or prior announcement, the titles of the specific sound recordings to be transmitted, the phonorecords embodying such sound recordings, or, other than for illustrative purposes, the names of the featured recording artists, except that this clause does not disqualify a transmitting entity that makes a prior announcement that a particular artist will be featured within an unspecified future time period, and in the case of a retransmission of a broadcast transmission by a transmitting entity that does not have the right or ability to control the programming of the broadcast transmission, the requirement of this clause shall not apply to a prior oral announcement by the broadcast station, or to an advance program schedule published, induced, or facilitated by the broadcast station, if the transmitting entity does not have actual knowledge and has not received written notice from the copyright owner or its representative that the broadcast station publishes or induces or facilitates the publication of such advance program schedule, or if such advance program schedule is a schedule of classical music programming published by the broadcast station in the same manner as published by that broadcast station on or before September 30, 1998;

'(iii) the transmission—

'(I) is not part of an archived program of less than 5 hours duration;

'(II) is not part of an archived program of 5 hours or greater in duration that is made available for a period exceeding 2 weeks;

'(III) is not part of a continuous program which is of less than 3 hours duration; or

'(IV) is not part of an identifiable program in which performances of sound recordings are rendered in a predetermined order, other than an archived or continuous program, that is transmitted at—

'(aa) more than 3 times in any 2-week period that have been publicly announced in advance, in the case of a program of less than 1 hour in duration, or

'(bb) more than 4 times in any 2-week period that have been publicly announced in advance, in the case of a program of 1 hour or more in duration,

except that the requirement of this subclause shall not apply in the case of a retransmission of a broadcast transmission by a transmitting entity that does not have the right or ability to control the programming of the broadcast transmission, unless the transmitting entity is given notice in writing by the copyright owner of the sound recording that the broadcast station makes broadcast transmissions that regularly violate such requirement;

'(iv) the transmitting entity does not knowingly perform the sound recording, as part of a service that offers transmissions of visual images contemporaneously with transmissions of sound recordings, in a manner that is likely to cause confusion, to cause mistake, or to deceive, as to the affiliation, connection, or association of the copyright owner or featured recording artist with the transmitting entity or a particular product or service advertised by the transmitting entity, or as to the origin, sponsorship, or approval by the copyright owner or featured recording artist of the activities of the transmitting entity other than the performance of the sound recording itself;

'(v) the transmitting entity cooperates to prevent, to the extent feasible without imposing substantial costs or burdens, a transmission recipient or any other person or entity from automatically scanning the transmitting entity's transmissions alone or together with transmissions by other transmitting entities in order to select a particular sound recording to be transmitted to the transmission recipient, except that the requirement of this clause shall not apply to a satellite digital audio service that is in operation, or that is licensed by the Federal Communications Commission, on or before July 31, 1998;

'(vi) the transmitting entity takes no affirmative steps to cause or induce the making of a phonorecord by the transmission recipient, and if the technology used by the transmitting entity enables the transmitting entity to limit the making by the transmission recipient of phonorecords of the transmission directly in a digital format, the transmitting entity sets such technology to limit such making of phonorecords to the extent permitted by such technology;

'(vii) phonorecords of the sound recording have been distributed to the public under the authority of the copyright owner or the copyright owner authorizes the transmitting entity to transmit the sound recording, and the transmitting entity makes the transmission from a phonorecord lawfully made under the authority of the copyright owner, except that the requirement of this clause shall not apply to a retransmission of a broadcast transmission by a transmitting entity that does not have the right or ability to control the programming of the broadcast transmission, unless the transmitting entity is given notice in writing by the copyright owner of the sound recording that the broadcast station makes broadcast transmissions that regularly violate such requirement;

'(viii) the transmitting entity accommodates and does not interfere with the transmission of technical measures that are widely used by sound recording copyright owners to identify or protect copyrighted works, and that are technically feasible of being transmitted by the transmitting entity without imposing substantial costs on the transmitting entity or resulting in perceptible aural or visual degradation of the digital signal, except that the requirement of this clause shall not apply to a satellite digital audio service that is in operation, or that is licensed under the authority of the Federal Communications Commission, on or before July 31, 1998, to the extent that such service has designed, developed, or made commitments to procure equipment or technology that is not compatible with such technical measures before such technical measures are widely adopted by sound recording copyright owners; and

'(ix) the transmitting entity identifies in textual data the sound recording during, but not before, the time it is performed, including the title of the sound recording, the title of the phonorecord embodying such sound recording, if any, and the featured recording artist, in a manner to permit it to be displayed to the transmission recipient by the device or technology intended for receiving the service provided by the transmitting entity, except that the obligation in this clause shall not take effect until 1 year after the date of the enactment of the Digital Millennium Copyright Act and shall not apply in the case of a retransmission of a broadcast transmission by a transmitting entity that does not have the right or ability to control the programming of the broadcast transmission, or in the case in which devices or technology intended for receiving the service provided by the transmitting entity that have the capability to display such textual data are not common in the marketplace.'.

(2) Subsection (f) is amended—

(A) in the subsection heading by striking 'NONEX-EMPT SUBSCRIPTION' and inserting 'CERTAIN NONEXEMPT';

(B) in paragraph (1)—

(i) in the first sentence—

(I) by striking '(1) No' and inserting '(1)(A) No';

(II) by striking 'the activities' and inserting 'subscription transmissions by preexisting subscription services and transmissions by preexisting satellite digital audio radio services'; and

(III) by striking '2000' and inserting '2001'; and

(ii) by amending the third sentence to read as follows: 'Any copyright owners of sound recordings, preexisting subscription services, or preexisting satellite digital audio radio services may submit to the Librarian of Congress licenses covering such subscription transmissions with respect to such sound recordings.'; and

(C) by striking paragraphs (2), (3), (4), and (5) and inserting the following:

'(B) In the absence of license agreements negotiated under subparagraph (A), during the 60-day period commencing 6 months after publication of the notice specified in subparagraph (A), and upon the filing of a petition in accordance with section 803(a)(1), the Librarian of Congress shall, pursuant to chapter 8, convene a copyright arbitration royalty panel to determine and publish in the Federal Register a schedule of rates and terms which, subject to paragraph (3), shall be binding on all copyright owners of sound recordings and entities performing sound recordings affected by this paragraph. In establishing rates and terms for preexisting subscription services and preexisting satellite digital audio radio services, in addition to the objectives set forth in section 801(b)(1), the copyright arbitration royalty panel may consider the rates and terms for comparable types of subscription digital audio transmission services and comparable circumstances under voluntary license agreements negotiated as provided in subparagraph (A).

'(C)(i) Publication of a notice of the initiation of voluntary negotiation proceedings as specified in subparagraph (A) shall be repeated, in accordance with regulations that the Librarian of Congress shall prescribe—

> '(I) no later than 30 days after a petition is filed by any copyright owners of sound recordings, any preexisting subscription services, or any preexisting satellite digital audio radio services indicating that a new type of subscription digital audio transmission service on which sound recordings are performed is or is about to become operational; and

> '(II) in the first week of January 2001, and at 5-year intervals thereafter.

'(ii) The procedures specified in subparagraph (B) shall be repeated, in accordance with regulations that the Librarian of

Congress shall prescribe, upon filing of a petition in accordance with section 803(a)(1) during a 60-day period commencing—

'(I) 6 months after publication of a notice of the initiation of voluntary negotiation proceedings under subparagraph (A) pursuant to a petition under clause (i)(I) of this subparagraph; or

'(II) on July 1, 2001, and at 5-year intervals thereafter.

'(iii) The procedures specified in subparagraph (B) shall be concluded in accordance with section 802.

'(2)(A) No later than 30 days after the date of the enactment of the Digital Millennium Copyright Act, the Librarian of Congress shall cause notice to be published in the Federal Register of the initiation of voluntary negotiation proceedings for the purpose of determining reasonable terms and rates of royalty payments for public performances of sound recordings by means of eligible nonsubscription transmissions and transmissions by new subscription services specified by subsection (d)(2) during the period beginning on the date of the enactment of such Act and ending on December 31, 2000, or such other date as the parties may agree. Such rates and terms shall distinguish among the different types of eligible nonsubscription transmission services and new subscription services then in operation and shall include a minimum fee for each such type of service. Any copyright owners of sound recordings or any entities performing sound recordings affected by this paragraph may submit to the Librarian of Congress licenses covering such eligible nonsubscription transmissions and new subscription services with respect to such sound recordings. The parties to each negotiation proceeding shall bear their own costs.

'(B) In the absence of license agreements negotiated under sub-paragraph (A), during the 60-day period commencing 6 months after publication of the notice specified in subparagraph (A), and upon the filing of a petition in accordance with section 803(a)(1), the Librarian of Congress shall, pursuant to chapter 8, convene a copyright arbitration royalty panel to determine and publish in the Federal Register a schedule of rates and terms which, subject to paragraph (3), shall be binding on all copyright owners of sound recordings and entities performing sound recordings affected by this paragraph during the period beginning on the date of the enactment of the Digital Millennium Copyright Act and ending on December 31, 2000, or such other date as the parties may agree. Such rates and terms shall distinguish among the different types of eligible nonsubscription transmission services then in operation and shall include a minimum fee for each such type of service, such differences to be based on criteria including, but not limited to, the quantity and nature of the use of sound recordings and the degree to which use of the service may substitute for or may promote the purchase of phonorecords by consumers. In establishing rates and terms for transmissions by eligible nonsubscription services and new subscription services, the copyright arbitration royalty panel shall establish rates and terms that most clearly represent the rates and terms that would have been negotiated in the marketplace between a willing buyer and a willing seller. In determining such rates and terms, the copyright arbitration royalty panel shall base its decision on economic, competitive and programming information presented by the parties, including—

'(i) whether use of the service may substitute for or may promote the sales of phonorecords or otherwise may interfere with or may enhance the sound recording copyright owner's other streams of revenue from its sound recordings; and

'(ii) the relative roles of the copyright owner and the transmitting entity in the copyrighted work and the service made available to the public with respect to relative creative contribution, technological contribution, capital investment, cost, and risk.

In establishing such rates and terms, the copyright arbitration royalty panel may consider the rates and terms for comparable types of digital audio transmission services and comparable circumstances under voluntary license agreements negotiated under subparagraph (A).

'(C)(i) Publication of a notice of the initiation of voluntary negotiation proceedings as specified in subparagraph (A) shall be repeated in accordance with regulations that the Librarian of Congress shall prescribe—

'(I) no later than 30 days after a petition is filed by any copyright owners of sound recordings or any eligible nonsubscription service or new subscription service indicating that a new type of eligible nonsubscription service or new subscription service on which sound recordings are performed is or is about to become operational; and

'(II) in the first week of January 2000, and at 2-year intervals thereafter, except to the extent that different years for the repeating of such proceedings may be determined in accordance with subparagraph (A).

'(ii) The procedures specified in subparagraph (B) shall be repeated, in accordance with regulations that the Librarian of Congress shall prescribe, upon filing of a petition in accordance with section 803(a)(1) during a 60-day period commencing—

'(I) 6 months after publication of a notice of the initiation of voluntary negotiation proceedings under subparagraph (A) pursuant to a petition under clause (i)(I); or

'(II) on July 1, 2000, and at 2-year intervals thereafter, except to the extent that different years for the repeating of such proceedings may be determined in accordance with subparagraph (A).

'(iii) The procedures specified in subparagraph (B) shall be concluded in accordance with section 802.

'(3) License agreements voluntarily negotiated at any time between 1 or more copyright owners of sound recordings and 1 or more entities performing sound recordings shall be given effect in lieu of any determination by a copyright arbitration royalty panel or decision by the Librarian of Congress.

'(4)(A) The Librarian of Congress shall also establish requirements by which copyright owners may receive reasonable notice of the use of their sound recordings under this section, and under which records of such use shall be kept and made available by entities performing sound recordings.

'(B) Any person who wishes to perform a sound recording publicly by means of a transmission eligible for statutory licensing under this subsection may do so without infringing the exclusive right of the copyright owner of the sound recording—

'(i) by complying with such notice requirements as the Librarian of Congress shall prescribe by regulation and by paying royalty fees in accordance with this subsection; or

'(ii) if such royalty fees have not been set, by agreeing to pay such royalty fees as shall be determined in accordance with this subsection.

'(C) Any royalty payments in arrears shall be made on or before the twentieth day of the month next succeeding the month in which the royalty fees are set.'.

(3) Subsection (g) is amended—

(A) in the subsection heading by striking 'SUB-SCRIP-TION';

(B) in paragraph (1) in the matter preceding subparagraph (A), by striking 'subscription transmission licensed' and inserting 'transmission licensed under a statutory license';

(C) in subparagraphs (A) and (B) by striking 'subscription'; and

(D) in paragraph (2) by striking 'subscription'.

(4) Subsection (j) is amended—

(A) by striking paragraphs (4) and (9) and redesignating paragraphs (2), (3), (5), (6), (7), and (8) as paragraphs (3), (5), (9), (12), (13), and (14), respectively;

(B) by inserting after paragraph (1) the following:

'(2) An 'archived program' is a predetermined program that is available repeatedly on the demand of the transmission recipient and that is performed in the same order from the beginning, except that an archived program shall not include a recorded event or broadcast transmission that makes no more than an incidental use of sound recordings, as long as such recorded event or broadcast transmission does not contain an entire sound recording or feature a particular sound recording.';

(C) by inserting after paragraph (3), as so redesignated, the following:

'(4) A 'continuous program' is a predetermined program that is continuously performed in the same order and that is accessed at a point in the program that is beyond the control of the transmission recipient.';

(D) by inserting after paragraph (5), as so redesignated, the following:

'(6) An 'eligible nonsubscription transmission' is a noninteractive nonsubscription digital audio transmission not exempt under subsection (d)(1) that is made as part of a service that provides audio programming consisting, in whole or in part, of performances of sound recordings, including retransmissions of broadcast transmissions, if the primary purpose of the service is to provide to the public such audio or other entertainment programming, and the primary purpose of the service is not to sell, advertise, or promote particular products or services other than sound recordings, live concerts, or other music-related events.

'(7) An 'interactive service' is one that enables a member of the public to receive a transmission of a program specially created for the recipient, or on request, a transmission of a particular sound recording, whether or not as part of a program, which is selected by or on behalf of the recipient. The ability of individuals to request that particular sound recordings be performed for reception by the public at large, or in the case of a subscription service, by all subscribers of the service, does not make a service interactive, if the programming on each channel of the service does not substantially consist of sound recordings that are performed within 1 hour of the request or at a time designated by either the transmitting entity or the individual making such request. If an entity offers both interactive and noninteractive services (either concurrently or at different times), the noninteractive component shall not be treated as part of an interactive service.

'(8) A 'new subscription service' is a service that performs sound recordings by means of noninteractive subscription digital audio transmissions and that is not a preexisting subscription service or a preexisting satellite digital audio radio service.';

    (E) by inserting after paragraph (9), as so redesignated, the following:

'(10) A 'preexisting satellite digital audio radio service' is a subscription satellite digital audio radio service provided pursuant to a satellite digital audio radio service license issued by the

Federal Communications Commission on or before July 31, 1998, and any renewal of such license to the extent of the scope of the original license, and may include a limited number of sample channels representative of the subscription service that are made available on a nonsubscription basis in order to promote the subscription service.

'(11) A 'preexisting subscription service' is a service that performs sound recordings by means of noninteractive audio-only subscription digital audio transmissions, which was in existence and was making such transmissions to the public for a fee on or before July 31, 1998, and may include a limited number of sample channels representative of the subscription service that are made available on a nonsubscription basis in order to promote the subscription service.'; and

(F) by adding at the end the following:

'(15) A 'transmission' is either an initial transmission or a retransmission.'.

(5) The amendment made by paragraph (2)(B)(i)(III) of this subsection shall be deemed to have been enacted as part of the Digital Performance Right in Sound Recordings Act of 1995, and the publication of notice of proceedings under section 114(f)(1) of title 17, United States Code, as in effect upon the effective date of that Act, for the determination of royalty payments shall be deemed to have been made for the period beginning on the effective date of that Act and ending on December 1, 2001.

(6) The amendments made by this subsection do not annul, limit, or otherwise impair the rights that are preserved by section

114 of title 17, United States Code, including the rights pre-served by subsections (c), (d)(4), and (i) of such section.

(b) EPHEMERAL RECORDINGS- Section 112 of title 17, United States Code, is amended—

(1) by redesignating subsection (e) as subsection (f); and

(2) by inserting after subsection (d) the following:

'(e) STATUTORY LICENSE- (1) A transmitting organization enti-tled to transmit to the public a performance of a sound recording under the limitation on exclusive rights specified by section 114(d)(1)(C)(iv) or under a statutory license in accordance with sec-tion 114(f) is entitled to a statutory license, under the conditions specified by this subsection, to make no more than 1 phonorecord of the sound recording (unless the terms and conditions of the statu-tory license allow for more), if the following conditions are satisfied:

'(A) The phonorecord is retained and used solely by the trans-mitting organization that made it, and no further phonorecords are reproduced from it.

'(B) The phonorecord is used solely for the transmitting organi-zation's own transmissions originating in the United States under a statutory license in accordance with section 114(f) or the limitation on exclusive rights specified by section 114(d)(1)(C)(iv).

'(C) Unless preserved exclusively for purposes of archival preservation, the phonorecord is destroyed within 6 months from the date the sound recording was first transmitted to the public using the phonorecord.

'(D) Phonorecords of the sound recording have been distributed to the public under the authority of the copyright owner or the copyright owner authorizes the transmitting entity to transmit the sound recording, and the transmitting entity makes the phonorecord under this subsection from a phonorecord lawfully made and acquired under the authority of the copyright owner.

'(3) Notwithstanding any provision of the antitrust laws, any copyright owners of sound recordings and any transmitting organizations entitled to a statutory license under this subsection may negotiate and agree upon royalty rates and license terms and conditions for making phonorecords of such sound recordings under this section and the proportionate division of fees paid among copyright owners, and may designate common agents to negotiate, agree to, pay, or receive such royalty payments.

'(4) No later than 30 days after the date of the enactment of the Digital Millennium Copyright Act, the Librarian of Congress shall cause notice to be published in the Federal Register of the initiation of voluntary negotiation proceedings for the purpose of determining reasonable terms and rates of royalty payments for the activities specified by paragraph (2) of this subsection during the period beginning on the date of the enactment of such Act and ending on December 31, 2000, or such other date as the parties may agree. Such rates shall include a minimum fee for each type of service offered by transmitting organizations. Any copyright owners of sound recordings or any transmitting organizations entitled to a statutory license under this subsection may submit to the Librarian of Congress licenses covering such activities with respect to such sound recordings. The parties to each negotiation proceeding shall bear their own costs.

'(5) In the absence of license agreements negotiated under paragraph (3), during the 60-day period commencing 6 months after publication of the notice specified in paragraph (4), and upon the filing of a petition in accordance with section 803(a)(1), the Librarian of Congress shall, pursuant to chapter 8, convene a copyright arbitration royalty panel to determine and publish in the Federal Register a schedule of reasonable rates and terms which, subject to paragraph (6), shall be binding on all copyright owners of sound recordings and transmitting organizations entitled to a statutory license under this subsection during the period beginning on the date of the enactment of the Digital Millennium Copyright Act and ending on December 31, 2000, or such other date as the parties may agree. Such rates shall include a minimum fee for each type of service offered by transmitting organizations. The copyright arbitration royalty panel shall establish rates that most clearly represent the fees that would have been negotiated in the marketplace between a willing buyer and a willing seller. In determining such rates and terms, the copyright arbitration royalty panel shall base its decision on economic, competitive, and programming information presented by the parties, including—

'(A) whether use of the service may substitute for or may promote the sales of phonorecords or otherwise interferes with or enhances the copyright owner's traditional streams of revenue; and

'(B) the relative roles of the copyright owner and the transmitting organization in the copyrighted work and the service made available to the public with respect to relative creative contribution, technological contribution, capital investment, cost, and risk.

In establishing such rates and terms, the copyright arbitration royalty panel may consider the rates and terms under voluntary license agreements negotiated as provided in paragraphs (3) and (4). The Librarian of Congress shall also establish requirements by which copyright owners may receive reasonable notice of the use of their sound recordings under this section, and under which records of such use shall be kept and made available by transmitting organizations entitled to obtain a statutory license under this subsection.

'(6) License agreements voluntarily negotiated at any time between 1 or more copyright owners of sound recordings and 1 or more transmitting organizations entitled to obtain a statutory license under this subsection shall be given effect in lieu of any determination by a copyright arbitration royalty panel or decision by the Librarian of Congress.

'(7) Publication of a notice of the initiation of voluntary negotiation proceedings as specified in paragraph (4) shall be repeated, in accordance with regulations that the Librarian of Congress shall prescribe, in the first week of January 2000, and at 2-year intervals thereafter, except to the extent that different years for the repeating of such proceedings may be determined in accordance with paragraph (4). The procedures specified in paragraph (5) shall be repeated, in accordance with regulations that the Librarian of Congress shall prescribe, upon filing of a petition in accordance with section 803(a)(1), during a 60-day period commencing on July 1, 2000, and at 2-year intervals thereafter, except to the extent that different years for the repeating of such proceedings may be determined in accordance with paragraph (4). The procedures specified in paragraph (5) shall be concluded in accordance with section 802.

'(8)(A) Any person who wishes to make a phonorecord of a sound recording under a statutory license in accordance with this subsection may do so without infringing the exclusive right of the copyright owner of the sound recording under section 106(1)—

'(i) by complying with such notice requirements as the Librarian of Congress shall prescribe by regulation and by paying royalty fees in accordance with this subsection; or

'(ii) if such royalty fees have not been set, by agreeing to pay such royalty fees as shall be determined in accordance with this subsection.

'(B) Any royalty payments in arrears shall be made on or before the 20th day of the month next succeeding the month in which the royalty fees are set.

'(9) If a transmitting organization entitled to make a phonorecord under this subsection is prevented from making such phonorecord by reason of the application by the copyright owner of technical measures that prevent the reproduction of the sound recording, the copyright owner shall make available to the transmitting organization the necessary means for permitting the making of such phonorecord as permitted under this subsection, if it is technologically feasible and economically reasonable for the copyright owner to do so. If the copyright owner fails to do so in a timely manner in light of the transmitting organization's reasonable business requirements, the transmitting organization shall not be liable for a violation of section 1201(a)(1) of this title for engaging in such activities as are necessary to make such phonorecords as permitted under this subsection.

'(10) Nothing in this subsection annuls, limits, impairs, or otherwise affects in any way the existence or value of any of the exclusive rights of the copyright owners in a sound recording, except as otherwise provided in this subsection, or in a musical work, including the exclusive rights to reproduce and distribute a sound recording or musical work, including by means of a digital phonorecord delivery, under sections 106(1), 106(3), and 115, and the right to perform publicly a sound recording or musical work, including by means of a digital audio transmission, under sections 106(4) and 106(6).'.

(c) SCOPE OF SECTION 112(a) OF TITLE 17 NOT AFFECTED- Nothing in this section or the amendments made by this section shall affect the scope of section 112(a) of title 17, United States Code, or the entitlement of any person to an exemption thereunder.

(d) PROCEDURAL AMENDMENTS TO CHAPTER 8- Section 802 of title 17, United States Code, is amended—

(1) in subsection (f)—

(A) in the first sentence by striking '60' and inserting '90'; and

(B) in the third sentence by striking 'that 60-day period' and inserting 'an additional 30-day period'; and

(2) in subsection (g) by inserting after the second sentence the following: 'When this title provides that the royalty rates or terms that were previously in effect are to expire on a specified date, any adjustment by the Librarian of those rates or terms shall be effective as of the day following the date of expiration of the rates or terms that were previously in effect, even if the Librarian's decision is rendered on a later date.'.

(e) CONFORMING AMENDMENTS- (1) Section 801(b)(1) of title 17, United States Code, is amended in the second sentence by striking 'sections 114, 115, and 116' and inserting 'sections 114(f)(1)(B), 115, and 116'.

(2) Section 802(c) of title 17, United States Code, is amended by striking 'section 111, 114, 116, or 119, any person entitled to a compulsory license' and inserting 'section 111, 112, 114, 116, or 119, any transmitting organization entitled to a statutory license under section 112(f), any person entitled to a statutory license'.

(3) Section 802(g) of title 17, United States Code, is amended by striking 'sections 111, 114' and inserting 'sections 111, 112, 114'.

(4) Section 802(h)(2) of title 17, United States Code, is amended by striking 'section 111, 114' and inserting 'section 111, 112, 114'.

(5) Section 803(a)(1) of title 17, United States Code, is amended by striking 'sections 114, 115' and inserting 'sections 112, 114, 115'.

(6) Section 803(a)(5) of title 17, United States Code, is amended—

(A) by striking 'section 114' and inserting 'section 112 or 114'; and

(B) by striking 'that section' and inserting 'those sections'.

## SEC. 406. ASSUMPTION OF CONTRACTUAL OBLIGATIONS RELATED TO TRANSFERS OF RIGHTS IN MOTION PICTURES.

(a) IN GENERAL- Part VI of title 28, United States Code, is amended by adding at the end the following new chapter:

## 'CHAPTER 180—ASSUMPTION OF CERTAIN CONTRACTUAL OBLIGATIONS

'Sec. 4001. Assumption of contractual obligations related to transfers of rights in motion pictures.

### 'Sec. 4001. Assumption of contractual obligations related to transfers of rights in motion pictures

'(a) ASSUMPTION OF OBLIGATIONS- (1) In the case of a transfer of copyright ownership under United States law in a motion picture (as the terms 'transfer of copyright ownership' and 'motion picture' are defined in section 101 of title 17) that is produced subject to 1 or more collective bargaining agreements negotiated under the laws of the United States, if the transfer is executed on or after the effective date of this chapter and is not limited to public performance rights, the transfer instrument shall be deemed to incorporate the assumption agreements applicable to the copyright ownership being transferred that are required by the applicable collective bargaining agreement, and the transferee shall be subject to the obligations under each such assumption agreement to make residual payments and provide related notices, accruing after the effective date of the transfer and applicable to the exploitation of the rights transferred, and any remedies under each such assumption agreement for breach of those obligations, as those obligations and remedies are set forth in the applicable collective bargaining agreement, if—

'(A) the transferee knows or has reason to know at the time of the transfer that such collective bargaining agreement was or will be applicable to the motion picture; or

'(B) in the event of a court order confirming an arbitration award against the transferor under the collective bargaining agreement, the transferor does not have the financial ability to satisfy the award within 90 days after the order is issued.

'(2) For purposes of paragraph (1)(A), 'knows or has reason to know' means any of the following:

'(A) Actual knowledge that the collective bargaining agreement was or will be applicable to the motion picture.

'(B)(i) Constructive knowledge that the collective bargaining agreement was or will be applicable to the motion picture, arising from recordation of a document pertaining to copyright in the motion picture under section 205 of title 17 or from publication, at a site available to the public on-line that is operated by the relevant union, of information that identifies the motion picture as subject to a collective bargaining agreement with that union, if the site permits commercially reasonable verification of the date on which the information was available for access.

'(ii) Clause (i) applies only if the transfer referred to in subsection (a)(1) occurs—

'(I) after the motion picture is completed, or

'(II) before the motion picture is completed and—

'(aa) within 18 months before the filing of an application for copyright registration for the motion picture under section 408 of title 17, or '(bb) if no such application is filed, within 18 months before the first publication of the motion picture in the United States.

'(C) Awareness of other facts and circumstances pertaining to a particular transfer from which it is apparent that the collective bargaining agreement was or will be applicable to the motion picture.

'(b) SCOPE OF EXCLUSION OF TRANSFERS OF PUBLIC PERFORMANCE RIGHTS- For purposes of this section, the exclusion under subsection (a) of transfers of copyright ownership in a motion picture that are limited to public performance rights includes transfers to a terrestrial broadcast station, cable system, or programmer to the extent that the station, system, or programmer is functioning as an exhibitor of the motion picture, either by exhibiting the motion picture on its own network, system, service, or station, or by initiating the transmission of an exhibition that is carried on another network, system, service, or station. When a terrestrial broadcast station, cable system, or programmer, or other transferee, is also functioning otherwise as a distributor or as a producer of the motion picture, the public performance exclusion does not affect any obligations imposed on the transferee to the extent that it is engaging in such functions.

'(c) EXCLUSION FOR GRANTS OF SECURITY INTERESTS- Subsection (a) shall not apply to—

'(1) a transfer of copyright ownership consisting solely of a mortgage, hypothecation, or other security interest; or

'(2) a subsequent transfer of the copyright ownership secured by the security interest described in paragraph (1) by or under the authority of the secured party, including a transfer through the exercise of the secured party's rights or remedies as a secured party, or by a subsequent transferee.

The exclusion under this subsection shall not affect any rights or remedies under law or contract.

'(d) DEFERRAL PENDING RESOLUTION OF BONA FIDE DISPUTE- A transferee on which obligations are imposed under subsection (a) by virtue of paragraph (1) of that subsection may elect to defer performance of such obligations that are subject to a bona fide dispute between a union and a prior transferor until that dispute is resolved, except that such deferral shall not stay accrual of any union claims due under an applicable collective bargaining agreement.

'(e) SCOPE OF OBLIGATIONS DETERMINED BY PRIVATE AGREEMENT- Nothing in this section shall expand or diminish the rights, obligations, or remedies of any person under the collective bargaining agreements or assumption agreements referred to in this section.

'(f) FAILURE TO NOTIFY- If the transferor under subsection (a) fails to notify the transferee under subsection (a) of applicable collective bargaining obligations before the execution of the transfer instrument, and subsection (a) is made applicable to the transferee solely by virtue of subsection (a)(1)(B), the transferor shall be liable to the transferee for any damages suffered by the transferee as a result of the failure to notify.

'(g) DETERMINATION OF DISPUTES AND CLAIMS- Any dispute concerning the application of subsections (a) through (f) shall be determined by an action in United States district court, and the court in its discretion may allow the recovery of full costs by or against any party and may also award a reasonable attorney's fee to the prevailing party as part of the costs.

'(h) STUDY- The Comptroller General, in consultation with the Register of Copyrights, shall conduct a study of the conditions in the motion picture industry that gave rise to this section, and the impact of this section on the motion picture industry. The Comptroller General shall report the findings of the study to the Congress within 2 years after the effective date of this chapter.'.

(b) CONFORMING AMENDMENT- The table of chapters for part VI of title 28, United States Code, is amended by adding at the end the following:

4001'.

## SEC. 407. EFFECTIVE DATE.

Except as otherwise provided in this title, this title and the amendments made by this title shall take effect on the date of the enactment of this Act.

## TITLE V—PROTECTION OF CERTAIN ORIGINAL DESIGNS

## SEC. 501. SHORT TITLE.

This Act may be referred to as the 'Vessel Hull Design Protection Act'.

## SEC. 502. PROTECTION OF CERTAIN ORIGINAL DESIGNS.

Title 17, United States Code, is amended by adding at the end the following new chapter:

## 'CHAPTER 13—PROTECTION OF ORIGINAL DESIGNS

'Sec.

'1301. Designs protected.

'1302. Designs not subject to protection.

'1303. Revisions, adaptations, and rearrangements.

'1304. Commencement of protection.

'1305. Term of protection.

'1306. Design notice.

'1307. Effect of omission of notice.

'1308. Exclusive rights.

'1309. Infringement.

'1310. Application for registration.

'1311. Benefit of earlier filing date in foreign country.

'1312. Oaths and acknowledgments.

'1313. Examination of application and issue or refusal of registration.

# 'Sec. 1301. Designs protected

'(a) DESIGNS PROTECTED-

'(1) IN GENERAL- The designer or other owner of an original design of a useful article which makes the article attractive or distinctive in appearance to the purchasing or using public may secure the protection provided by this chapter upon complying with and subject to this chapter.

'(2) VESSEL HULLS- The design of a vessel hull, including a plug or mold, is subject to protection under this chapter, notwithstanding section 1302(4).

'(b) DEFINITIONS- For the purpose of this chapter, the following terms have the following meanings:

'(1) A design is 'original' if it is the result of the designer's creative endeavor that provides a distinguishable variation over prior work pertaining to similar articles which is more than merely trivial and has not been copied from another source.

'(2) A 'useful article' is a vessel hull, including a plug or mold, which in normal use has an intrinsic utilitarian function that is not merely to portray the appearance of the article or to convey information. An article which normally is part of a useful article shall be deemed to be a useful article.

'(3) A 'vessel' is a craft, especially one larger than a rowboat, designed to navigate on water, but does not include any such craft that exceeds 200 feet in length.

'(4) A 'hull' is the frame or body of a vessel, including the deck of a vessel, exclusive of masts, sails, yards, and rigging.

'(5) A 'plug' means a device or model used to make a mold for the purpose of exact duplication, regardless of whether the device or model has an intrinsic utilitarian function that is not only to portray the appearance of the product or to convey information.

'(6) A 'mold' means a matrix or form in which a substance for material is used, regardless of whether the matrix or form has an intrinsic utilitarian function that is not only to portray the appearance of the product or to convey information.

## 'Sec. 1302. Designs not subject to protection

'Protection under this chapter shall not be available for a design that is—

'(1) not original;

'(2) staple or commonplace, such as a standard geometric figure, a familiar symbol, an emblem, or a motif, or another shape, pattern, or configuration which has become standard, common, prevalent, or ordinary;

'(3) different from a design excluded by paragraph (2) only in insignificant details or in elements which are variants commonly used in the relevant trades;

'(4) dictated solely by a utilitarian function of the article that embodies it; or

'(5) embodied in a useful article that was made public by the designer or owner in the United States or a foreign country more than 1 year before the date of the application for registration under this chapter.

### 'Sec. 1303. Revisions, adaptations, and rearrangements

'Protection for a design under this chapter shall be available notwithstanding the employment in the design of subject matter excluded from protection under section 1302 if the design is a substantial revision, adaptation, or rearrangement of such subject matter. Such protection shall be independent of any subsisting protection in subject matter employed in the design, and shall not be construed as securing any right to subject matter excluded from protection under this chapter or as extending any subsisting protection under this chapter.

### 'Sec. 1304. Commencement of protection

'The protection provided for a design under this chapter shall commence upon the earlier of the date of publication of the registration under section 1313(a) or the date the design is first made public as defined by section 1310(b).

### 'Sec. 1305. Term of protection

'(a) IN GENERAL- Subject to subsection (b), the protection provided under this chapter for a design shall continue for a term of 10 years beginning on the date of the commencement of protection under section 1304.

'(b) EXPIRATION- All terms of protection provided in this section shall run to the end of the calendar year in which they would otherwise expire.

'(c) TERMINATION OF RIGHTS- Upon expiration or termination of protection in a particular design under this chapter, all rights under this chapter in the design shall terminate, regardless of the number of different articles in which the design may have been used during the term of its protection.

## 'Sec. 1306. Design notice

'(a) CONTENTS OF DESIGN NOTICE- (1) Whenever any design for which protection is sought under this chapter is made public under section 1310(b), the owner of the design shall, subject to the provisions of section 1307, mark it or have it marked legibly with a design notice consisting of—

'(A) the words 'Protected Design', the abbreviation 'Prot'd Des.', or the letter 'D' with a circle, or the symbol '*D*';

'(B) the year of the date on which protection for the design commenced; and

'(C) the name of the owner, an abbreviation by which the name can be recognized, or a generally accepted alternative designation of the owner.

Any distinctive identification of the owner may be used for purposes of subparagraph (C) if it has been recorded by the Administrator before the design marked with such identification is registered.

'(2) After registration, the registration number may be used instead of the elements specified in subparagraphs (B) and (C) of paragraph (1).

'(b) LOCATION OF NOTICE- The design notice shall be so located and applied as to give reasonable notice of design protection while the useful article embodying the design is passing through its normal channels of commerce.

'(c) SUBSEQUENT REMOVAL OF NOTICE- When the owner of a design has complied with the provisions of this section, protection under this chapter shall not be affected by the removal, destruction, or obliteration by others of the design notice on an article.

### 'Sec. 1307. Effect of omission of notice

'(a) ACTIONS WITH NOTICE- Except as provided in subsection (b), the omission of the notice prescribed in section 1306 shall not cause loss of the protection under this chapter or prevent recovery for infringement under this chapter against any person who, after receiving written notice of the design protection, begins an undertaking leading to infringement under this chapter.

'(b) ACTIONS WITHOUT NOTICE- The omission of the notice prescribed in section 1306 shall prevent any recovery under section 1323 against a person who began an undertaking leading to infringement under this chapter before receiving written notice of the design protection. No injunction shall be issued under this chapter with respect to such undertaking unless the owner of the design reimburses that person for any reasonable expenditure or contractual obligation in connection with such undertaking that was incurred before receiving written notice of the design protection, as the court in its discretion directs. The burden of providing written notice of design protection shall be on the owner of the design.

### 'Sec. 1308. Exclusive rights

'The owner of a design protected under this chapter has the exclusive right to—

'(1) make, have made, or import, for sale or for use in trade, any useful article embodying that design; and

'(2) sell or distribute for sale or for use in trade any useful article embodying that design.

## 'Sec. 1309. Infringement

'(a) ACTS OF INFRINGEMENT- Except as provided in subsection (b), it shall be infringement of the exclusive rights in a design protected under this chapter for any person, without the consent of the owner of the design, within the United States and during the term of such protection, to—

'(1) make, have made, or import, for sale or for use in trade, any infringing article as defined in subsection (e); or

'(2) sell or distribute for sale or for use in trade any such infringing article.

'(b) ACTS OF SELLERS AND DISTRIBUTORS- A seller or distributor of an infringing article who did not make or import the article shall be deemed to have infringed on a design protected under this chapter only if that person—

'(1) induced or acted in collusion with a manufacturer to make, or an importer to import such article, except that merely purchasing or giving an order to purchase such article in the ordinary course of business shall not of itself constitute such inducement or collusion; or

'(2) refused or failed, upon the request of the owner of the design, to make a prompt and full disclosure of that person's source of such article, and that person orders or reorders such article after receiving notice by registered or certified mail of the protection subsisting in the design.

'(c) ACTS WITHOUT KNOWLEDGE- It shall not be infringement under this section to make, have made, import, sell, or distribute, any article embodying a design which was created without
knowledge that a design was protected under this chapter and was
copied from such protected design.

'(d) ACTS IN ORDINARY COURSE OF BUSINESS- A person
who incorporates into that person's product of manufacture an
infringing article acquired from others in the ordinary course of
business, or who, without knowledge of the protected design
embodied in an infringing article, makes or processes the infringing
article for the account of another person in the ordinary course of
business, shall not be deemed to have infringed the rights in that
design under this chapter except under a condition contained in
paragraph (1) or (2) of subsection (b). Accepting an order or reorder
from the source of the infringing article shall be deemed ordering or
reordering within the meaning of subsection (b)(2).

'(e) INFRINGING ARTICLE DEFINED- As used in this section,
an 'infringing article' is any article the design of which has been
copied from a design protected under this chapter, without the consent of the owner of the protected design. An infringing article is not
an illustration or picture of a protected design in an advertisement,
book, periodical, newspaper, photograph, broadcast, motion picture, or similar medium. A design shall not be deemed to have been
copied from a protected design if it is original and not substantially
similar in appearance to a protected design.

'(f) ESTABLISHING ORIGINALITY- The party to any action or
proceeding under this chapter who alleges rights under this chapter
in a design shall have the burden of establishing the design's original-
ity whenever the opposing party introduces an earlier work which is

identical to such design, or so similar as to make prima facie showing that such design was copied from such work.

'(g) REPRODUCTION FOR TEACHING OR ANALYSIS- It is not an infringement of the exclusive rights of a design owner for a person to reproduce the design in a useful article or in any other form solely for the purpose of teaching, analyzing, or evaluating the appearance, concepts, or techniques embodied in the design, or the function of the useful article embodying the design.

### 'Sec. 1310. Application for registration

'(a) TIME LIMIT FOR APPLICATION FOR REGISTRATION- Protection under this chapter shall be lost if application for registration of the design is not made within 2 years after the date on which the design is first made public.

'(b) WHEN DESIGN IS MADE PUBLIC- A design is made public when an existing useful article embodying the design is anywhere publicly exhibited, publicly distributed, or offered for sale or sold to the public by the owner of the design or with the owner's consent.

'(c) APPLICATION BY OWNER OF DESIGN- Application for registration may be made by the owner of the design.

'(d) CONTENTS OF APPLICATION- The application for registration shall be made to the Administrator and shall state—

'(1) the name and address of the designer or designers of the design;

'(2) the name and address of the owner if different from the designer;

'(3) the specific name of the useful article embodying the design;

'(4) the date, if any, that the design was first made public, if such date was earlier than the date of the application;

'(5) affirmation that the design has been fixed in a useful article; and

'(6) such other information as may be required by the Administrator.

The application for registration may include a description setting forth the salient features of the design, but the absence of such a description shall not prevent registration under this chapter.

'(e) SWORN STATEMENT- The application for registration shall be accompanied by a statement under oath by the applicant or the applicant's duly authorized agent or representative, setting forth, to the best of the applicant's knowledge and belief—

'(1) that the design is original and was created by the designer or designers named in the application;

'(2) that the design has not previously been registered on behalf of the applicant or the applicant's predecessor in title; and

'(3) that the applicant is the person entitled to protection and to registration under this chapter.

If the design has been made public with the design notice prescribed in section 1306, the statement shall also describe the exact form and position of the design notice.

'(f) EFFECT OF ERRORS- (1) Error in any statement or assertion as to the utility of the useful article named in the application under this section, the design of which is sought to be registered, shall not affect the protection secured under this chapter.

'(2) Errors in omitting a joint designer or in naming an alleged joint designer shall not affect the validity of the registration, or the actual ownership or the protection of the design, unless it is shown that the error occurred with deceptive intent.

'(g) DESIGN MADE IN SCOPE OF EMPLOYMENT- In a case in which the design was made within the regular scope of the designer's employment and individual authorship of the design is difficult or impossible to ascribe and the application so states, the name and address of the employer for whom the design was made may be stated instead of that of the individual designer.

'(h) PICTORIAL REPRESENTATION OF DESIGN- The application for registration shall be accompanied by two copies of a drawing or other pictorial representation of the useful article embodying the design, having one or more views, adequate to show the design, in a form and style suitable for reproduction, which shall be deemed a part of the application.

'(i) DESIGN IN MORE THAN ONE USEFUL ARTICLE- If the distinguishing elements of a design are in substantially the same form in different useful articles, the design shall be protected as to all such useful articles when protected as to one of them, but not more than one registration shall be required for the design.

'(j) APPLICATION FOR MORE THAN ONE DESIGN- More than one design may be included in the same application under such conditions as may be prescribed by the Administrator. For each design included in an application the fee prescribed for a single design shall be paid.

## 'Sec. 1311. Benefit of earlier filing date in foreign country

'An application for registration of a design filed in the United States by any person who has, or whose legal representative or predecessor or successor in title has, previously filed an application for registration of the same design in a foreign country which extends to designs of owners who are citizens of the United States, or to applications filed under this chapter, similar protection to that provided under this chapter shall have that same effect as if filed in the United States on the date on which the application was first filed in such foreign country, if the application in the United States is filed within 6 months after the earliest date on which any such foreign application was filed.

## 'Sec. 1312. Oaths and acknowledgments

'(a) IN GENERAL- Oaths and acknowledgments required by this chapter—

'(1) may be made—

'(A) before any person in the United States authorized by law to administer oaths; or

'(B) when made in a foreign country, before any diplomatic or consular officer of the United States authorized to administer oaths, or before any official authorized to administer oaths in the foreign country concerned, whose authority shall be proved by a certificate of a diplomatic or consular officer of the United States; and

'(2) shall be valid if they comply with the laws of the State or country where made.

'(b) WRITTEN DECLARATION IN LIEU OF OATH- (1) The Administrator may by rule prescribe that any document which is to be filed under this chapter in the Office of the Administrator and which is required by any law, rule, or other regulation to be under oath, may be subscribed to by a written declaration in such form as the Administrator may prescribe, and such declaration shall be in lieu of the oath otherwise required.

'(2) Whenever a written declaration under paragraph (1) is used, the document containing the declaration shall state that willful false statements are punishable by fine or imprisonment, or both, pursuant to section 1001 of title 18, and may jeopardize the validity of the application or document or a registration resulting therefrom.

## 'Sec. 1313. Examination of application and issue or refusal of registration

'(a) DETERMINATION OF REGISTRABILITY OF DESIGN; REGISTRATION- Upon the filing of an application for registration in proper form under section 1310, and upon payment of the fee prescribed under section 1316, the Administrator shall determine whether or not the application relates to a design which on its face appears to be subject to protection under this chapter, and, if so, the Register shall register the design. Registration under this subsection shall be announced by publication. The date of registration shall be the date of publication.

'(b) REFUSAL TO REGISTER; RECONSIDERATION- If, in the judgment of the Administrator, the application for registration relates to a design which on its face is not subject to protection under this chapter, the Administrator shall send to the applicant a notice of refusal to register and the grounds for the refusal. Within 3 months after the date on which the notice of refusal is sent, the applicant may, by written request, seek reconsideration of the application. After consideration of such a request, the Administrator shall either register the design or send to the applicant a notice of final refusal to register.

'(c) APPLICATION TO CANCEL REGISTRATION- Any person who believes he or she is or will be damaged by a registration under this chapter may, upon payment of the prescribed fee, apply to the Administrator at any time to cancel the registration on the ground that the design is not subject to protection under this chapter, stating the reasons for the request. Upon receipt of an application for cancellation, the Administrator shall send to the owner of the design, as shown in the records of the Office of the Administrator, a notice of the application, and the owner shall have a period of 3 months after the date on which such notice is mailed in which to present arguments to the Administrator for support of the validity of the registration. The Administrator shall also have the authority to establish, by regulation, conditions under which the opposing parties may appear and be heard in support of their arguments. If, after the periods provided for the presentation of arguments have expired, the Administrator determines that the applicant for cancellation has established that the design is not subject to protection under this chapter, the Administrator shall order the registration stricken from the record. Cancellation under this subsection shall be announced by publication, and notice of the Administrator's final determination with respect to any application for cancellation shall be sent to the applicant and to the owner of record.

## 'Sec. 1314. Certification of registration

'Certificates of registration shall be issued in the name of the United States under the seal of the Office of the Administrator and shall be recorded in the official records of the Office. The certificate shall state the name of the useful article, the date of filing of the application, the date of registration, and the date the design was made public, if earlier than the date of filing of the application, and shall contain a reproduction of the drawing or other pictorial representation of the design. If a description of the salient features of the design appears in the application, the description shall also appear in the certificate. A certificate of registration shall be admitted in any court as prima facie evidence of the facts stated in the certificate.

## 'Sec. 1315. Publication of announcements and indexes

'(a) PUBLICATIONS OF THE ADMINISTRATOR- The Administrator shall publish lists and indexes of registered designs and cancellations of designs and may also publish the drawings or other pictorial representations of registered designs for sale or other distribution.

'(b) FILE OF REPRESENTATIVES OF REGISTERED DESIGNS- The Administrator shall establish and maintain a file of the drawings or other pictorial representations of registered designs. The file shall be available for use by the public under such conditions as the Administrator may prescribe.

## 'Sec. 1316. Fees

'The Administrator shall by regulation set reasonable fees for the filing of applications to register designs under this chapter and for other services relating to the administration of this chapter, taking into consideration the cost of providing these services and the benefit of a public record.

## 'Sec. 1317. Regulations

'The Administrator may establish regulations for the administration of this chapter.

## 'Sec. 1318. Copies of records

'Upon payment of the prescribed fee, any person may obtain a certified copy of any official record of the Office of the Administrator that relates to this chapter. That copy shall be admissible in evidence with the same effect as the original.

## 'Sec. 1319. Correction of errors in certificates

'The Administrator may, by a certificate of correction under seal, correct any error in a registration incurred through the fault of the Office, or, upon payment of the required fee, any error of a clerical or typographical nature occurring in good faith but not through the fault of the Office. Such registration, together with the certificate, shall thereafter have the same effect as if it had been originally issued in such corrected form.

## 'Sec. 1320. Ownership and transfer

'(a) PROPERTY RIGHT IN DESIGN- The property right in a design subject to protection under this chapter shall vest in the designer, the legal representatives of a deceased designer or of one under legal incapacity, the employer for whom the designer created the design in the case of a design made within the regular scope of the designer's employment, or a person to whom the rights of the designer or of such employer have been transferred. The person in whom the property right is vested shall be considered the owner of the design.

'(b) TRANSFER OF PROPERTY RIGHT- The property right in a registered design, or a design for which an application for registration has been or may be filed, may be assigned, granted, conveyed, or mortgaged by an instrument in writing, signed by the owner, or may be bequeathed by will.

'(c) OATH OR ACKNOWLEDGEMENT OF TRANSFER- An oath or acknowledgment under section 1312 shall be prima facie evidence of the execution of an assignment, grant, conveyance, or mortgage under subsection (b).

'(d) RECORDATION OF TRANSFER- An assignment, grant, conveyance, or mortgage under subsection (b) shall be void as against any subsequent purchaser or mortgagee for a valuable consideration, unless it is recorded in the Office of the Administrator within 3 months after its date of execution or before the date of such subsequent purchase or mortgage.

## 'Sec. 1321. Remedy for infringement

'(a) IN GENERAL- The owner of a design is entitled, after issuance of a certificate of registration of the design under this chapter, to institute an action for any infringement of the design.

'(b) REVIEW OF REFUSAL TO REGISTER- (1) Subject to paragraph (2), the owner of a design may seek judicial review of a final refusal of the Administrator to register the design under this chapter by bringing a civil action, and may in the same action, if the court adjudges the design subject to protection under this chapter, enforce the rights in that design under this chapter.

'(2) The owner of a design may seek judicial review under this section if—

'(A) the owner has previously duly filed and prosecuted to final refusal an application in proper form for registration of the design;

'(B) the owner causes a copy of the complaint in the action to be delivered to the Administrator within 10 days after the commencement of the action; and

'(C) the defendant has committed acts in respect to the design which would constitute infringement with respect to a design protected under this chapter.

'(c) ADMINISTRATOR AS PARTY TO ACTION- The Administrator may, at the Administrator's option, become a party to the action with respect to the issue of registrability of the design claim by entering an appearance within 60 days after being served with the complaint, but the failure of the Administrator to become a party shall not deprive the court of jurisdiction to determine that issue.

'(d) USE OF ARBITRATION TO RESOLVE DISPUTE- The parties to an infringement dispute under this chapter, within such time as may be specified by the Administrator by regulation, may determine the dispute, or any aspect of the dispute, by arbitration. Arbitration shall be governed by title 9. The parties shall give notice of any arbitration award to the Administrator, and such award shall, as between the parties to the arbitration, be dispositive of the issues to which it relates. The arbitration award shall be unenforceable until such notice is given. Nothing in this subsection shall preclude the Administrator from determining whether a design is subject to registration in a cancellation proceeding under section 1313(c).

## Sec. 1322. Injunctions

'(a) IN GENERAL- A court having jurisdiction over actions under this chapter may grant injunctions in accordance with the principles of equity to prevent infringement of a design under this chapter, including, in its discretion, prompt relief by temporary restraining orders and preliminary injunctions.

'(b) DAMAGES FOR INJUNCTIVE RELIEF WRONGFULLY OBTAINED- A seller or distributor who suffers damage by reason of injunctive relief wrongfully obtained under this section has a cause of action against the applicant for such injunctive relief and may recover such relief as may be appropriate, including damages for lost profits, cost of materials, loss of good will, and punitive damages in instances where the injunctive relief was sought in bad faith, and, unless the court finds extenuating circumstances, reasonable attorney's fees.

## 'Sec. 1323. Recovery for infringement

'(a) DAMAGES- Upon a finding for the claimant in an action for infringement under this chapter, the court shall award the claimant damages adequate to compensate for the infringement. In addition, the court may increase the damages to such amount, not exceeding $50,000 or $1 per copy, whichever is greater, as the court determines to be just. The damages awarded shall constitute compensation and not a penalty. The court may receive expert testimony as an aid to the determination of damages.

'(b) INFRINGER'S PROFITS- As an alternative to the remedies provided in subsection (a), the court may award the claimant the infringer's profits resulting from the sale of the copies if the court finds that the infringer's sales are reasonably related to the use of the claimant's design. In such a case, the claimant shall be required to prove only the amount of the infringer's sales and the infringer shall be required to prove its expenses against such sales.

'(c) STATUTE OF LIMITATIONS- No recovery under subsection (a) or (b) shall be had for any infringement committed more than 3 years before the date on which the complaint is filed.

'(d) ATTORNEY'S FEES- In an action for infringement under this chapter, the court may award reasonable attorney's fees to the prevailing party.

'(e) DISPOSITION OF INFRINGING AND OTHER ARTICLES- The court may order that all infringing articles, and any plates, molds, patterns, models, or other means specifically adapted for making the articles, be delivered up for destruction or other disposition as the court may direct.

## 'Sec. 1324. Power of court over registration

'In any action involving the protection of a design under this chapter, the court, when appropriate, may order registration of a design under this chapter or the cancellation of such a registration. Any such order shall be certified by the court to the Administrator, who shall make an appropriate entry upon the record.

### 'Sec. 1325. Liability for action on registration fraudulently obtained

'Any person who brings an action for infringement knowing that registration of the design was obtained by a false or fraudulent representation materially affecting the rights under this chapter, shall be liable in the sum of $10,000, or such part of that amount as the court may determine. That amount shall be to compensate the defendant and shall be charged against the plaintiff and paid to the defendant, in addition to such costs and attorney's fees of the defendant as may be assessed by the court.

### 'Sec. 1326. Penalty for false marking

'(a) IN GENERAL- Whoever, for the purpose of deceiving the public, marks upon, applies to, or uses in advertising in connection with an article made, used, distributed, or sold, a design which is not protected under this chapter, a design notice specified in section 1306, or any other words or symbols importing that the design is protected under this chapter, knowing that the design is not so protected, shall pay a civil fine of not more than $500 for each such offense.

'(b) SUIT BY PRIVATE PERSONS- Any person may sue for the penalty established by subsection (a), in which event one-half of the penalty shall be awarded to the person suing and the remainder shall be awarded to the United States.

### 'Sec. 1327. Penalty for false representation

'Whoever knowingly makes a false representation materially affecting the rights obtainable under this chapter for the purpose of obtaining registration of a design under this chapter shall pay a penalty of not less than $500 and not more than $1,000, and any rights or privileges that individual may have in the design under this chapter shall be forfeited.

## 'Sec. 1328. Enforcement by Treasury and Postal Service

'(a) REGULATIONS- The Secretary of the Treasury and the United States Postal Service shall separately or jointly issue regulations for the enforcement of the rights set forth in section 1308 with respect to importation. Such regulations may require, as a condition for the exclusion of articles from the United States, that the person seeking exclusion take any one or more of the following actions:

'(1) Obtain a court order enjoining, or an order of the International Trade Commission under section 337 of the Tariff Act of 1930 excluding, importation of the articles.

'(2) Furnish proof that the design involved is protected under this chapter and that the importation of the articles would infringe the rights in the design under this chapter.

'(3) Post a surety bond for any injury that may result if the detention or exclusion of the articles proves to be unjustified.

'(b) SEIZURE AND FORFEITURE- Articles imported in violation of the rights set forth in section 1308 are subject to seizure and forfeiture in the same manner as property imported in violation of the customs laws. Any such forfeited articles shall be destroyed as directed by the Secretary of the Treasury or the court, as the case may be, except that the articles may be returned to the country of export whenever it is shown to the satisfaction of the Secretary of the Treasury that the importer had no reasonable grounds for believing that his or her acts constituted a violation of the law.

### 'Sec. 1329. Relation to design patent law

'The issuance of a design patent under title 35, United States Code, for an original design for an article of manufacture shall terminate any protection of the original design under this chapter.

### 'Sec. 1330. Common law and other rights unaffected

'Nothing in this chapter shall annul or limit—

'(1) common law or other rights or remedies, if any, available to or held by any person with respect to a design which has not been registered under this chapter; or

'(2) any right under the trademark laws or any right protected against unfair competition.

### 'Sec. 1331. Administrator; Office of the Administrator

'In this chapter, the 'Administrator' is the Register of Copyrights, and the 'Office of the Administrator' and the 'Office' refer to the Copyright Office of the Library of Congress.

### 'Sec. 1332. No retroactive effect

'Protection under this chapter shall not be available for any design that has been made public under section 1310(b) before the effective date of this chapter.'.

### SEC. 503. CONFORMING AMENDMENTS.

(a) TABLE OF CHAPTERS- The table of chapters for title 17, United States Code, is amended by adding at the end the following:

**1301'.**

(b) JURISDICTION OF DISTRICT COURTS OVER DESIGN ACTIONS- (1) Section 1338(c) of title 28, United States Code, is amended by inserting ', and to exclusive rights in designs under chapter 13 of title 17,' after 'title 17'.

(2)(A) The section heading for section 1338 of title 28, United States Code, is amended by inserting '**designs,**' after '**mask works,**'.

(B) The item relating to section 1338 in the table of sections at the beginning of chapter 85 of title 28, United States Code, is amended by inserting 'designs,' after 'mask works,'.

(c) PLACE FOR BRINGING DESIGN ACTIONS- (1) Section 1400(a) of title 28, United States Code, is amended by inserting 'or designs' after 'mask works'.

(2) The section heading for section 1400 of title 28, United States Code, is amended to read as follows:

'**Patents and copyrights, mask works, and designs**'.

(3) The item relating to section 1400 in the table of sections at the beginning of chapter 87 of title 28, United States Code, is amended to read as follows:

'1400. Patents and copyrights, mask works, and designs.'.

(d) ACTIONS AGAINST THE UNITED STATES- Section 1498(e) of title 28, United States Code, is amended by inserting ', and to exclusive rights in designs under chapter 13 of title 17,' after 'title 17'.

## SEC. 504. JOINT STUDY OF THE EFFECT OF THIS TITLE.

(a) IN GENERAL- Not later than 1 year after the date of the enactment of this Act, and not later than 2 years after such date of enactment, the Register of Copyrights and the Commissioner of Patents and Trademarks shall submit to the Committees on the Judiciary of the Senate and the House of Representatives a joint report evaluating the effect of the amendments made by this title.

(b) ELEMENTS FOR CONSIDERATION- In carrying out subsection (a), the Register of Copyrights and the Commissioner of Patents and Trademarks shall consider—

(1) the extent to which the amendments made by this title has been effective in suppressing infringement of the design of vessel hulls;

(2) the extent to which the registration provided for in chapter 13 of title 17, United States Code, as added by this title, has been utilized;

(3) the extent to which the creation of new designs of vessel hulls have been encouraged by the amendments made by this title;

(4) the effect, if any, of the amendments made by this title on the price of vessels with hulls protected under such amendments; and

(5) such other considerations as the Register and the Commissioner may deem relevant to accomplish the purposes of the evaluation conducted under subsection (a).

## SEC. 505. EFFECTIVE DATE.

The amendments made by sections 502 and 503 shall take effect on the date of the enactment of this Act and shall remain in effect until the end of the 2-year period beginning on such date of enactment. No cause of action based on chapter 13 of title 17, United States Code, as added by this title, may be filed after the end of that 2-year period.

Speaker of the House of Representatives.
Vice President of the United States and
President of the Senate.

# *Appendix IV*
# *Amicus Brief*

Brief *amicus curiae* filed by participants in the *Openlaw/DVD* <*http://eon.law.harvard.edu/openlaw/DVD/*> forum, May 30, 2000.

UNITED STATES DISTRICT COURT
SOUTHERN DISTRICT OF NEW YORK

---

UNIVERSAL CITY STUDIOS, INC.,
PARAMOUNT PICTURES CORPORATION,
METRO-GOLDWYN-MAYER STUDIOS INC.,
TRISTAR PICTURES, INC.,
COLUMBIA PICTURES INDUSTRIES, INC.,
TIME WARNER ENTERTAINMENT CO.,
L.P., DISNEY ENTERPRISES, INC.,
and TWENTIETH CENTURY FOX FILM CORPORATION,
Plaintiffs,

-against- ERIC CORLEY a/k/a "EMMANUEL GOLDSTEIN"
and 2600 ENTERPRISES, INC., Defendants Case No.: 00 Civ.
0277 (LAK)

**BRIEF OF OPENLAW PARTICIPANTS
AS *AMICUS CURIAE* IN SUPPORT OF DEFENDANTS
ERIC CORLEY, a/k/a "EMMANUEL GOLDSTEIN" AND
2600 ENTERPRISES**

The undersigned participants in the Openlaw/DVD forum respectfully submit this brief *amicus curiae* in opposition to plaintiffs' motion to modify the preliminary injunction and in support of defendant's motion to vacate the injunction.

## Preliminary Statement

Plaintiffs seek to extend the Court's preliminary injunction to prohibit *2600* magazine from publishing a hyperlinked account of and commentary on its ongoing legal battle. They ask this Court to suppress speech on the unproven assertion that the speech constitutes "providing" of what is alleged, but again not proven to be, a circumvention device. The Court should reject this extraordinary prior restraint and, on the fuller record now available, should vacate the existing injunction.

*2600*'s website does not provide a circumvention device. It provides commentary on the Digital Millennium Copyright Act's ("DMCA") anticircumvention provisions, criticism of plaintiffs' legal tactics, and information about DeCSS, but it does not provide DeCSS. Instead, *2600* uses the speech-enhancing technologies of the Web to engage its readers in a dialogue about anticircumvention and censorship. Hyperlinks are the very core of the Web, and an integral part of online dialogue about this case, connecting readers of *2600* with other supporters of the magazine and their political statements. As such, hyperlinks are expression that demands the full range of First Amendment protection.

Plaintiffs demand the suppression of this hyperlink speech based on its content, a position clearly offensive to the First Amendment. The proposed injunction would chill not only *2600*'s speech, but that of hundreds of third parties. Plaintiffs would have this Court examine the pages at the other end of every link on *2600*'s website and, by barring those links the targets of which plaintiffs found objectionable, prevent *2600*'s readers from communicating easily with those sites. The First Amendment prevents this Court from aiding plaintiffs in that endeavor.

Plaintiffs' attempt to reach links under theories of contributory liability must likewise fail. The anti-distribution provisions of §1201(a)(2) and (b)(2) already reach the limits of contributory copyright infringement. Plaintiffs overreach when they try to add on top of that a contributory "paracopyright" violation. Concerns for the protection of speech should join the knowledge, intent, and foreseeability requirements of tort law to preclude from the imposition of liability on alleged violators twice removed from any potential copyright infringement.

## Interests of Amici

As authors, developers, and users of the World Wide Web, and as students, teachers, and researchers, we write to address the threat to online speech that the proposed injunction against hyperlinking would pose. If anyone on the Internet can become a "town crier," everyone gains a newsroom, a research library, a university, a laboratory. *See Reno v. American Civil Liberties Union*, 521 U.S. 844, 870 117 S.Ct. 2329, 2344 (1997). The proposed injunction would cripple all of these. The Internet allows people to interact in a wide range of roles only if its lines of communication—its hyperlinks—remain open. Plaintiffs' motion to close these links, like their interpretation of the anticircumvention provision, would deny access to information.

Hyperlinks, by facilitating access to information, give the Web its vitality as a communications network. Using hyperlinks, a professor's syllabus draws on current news and research; a journalist adds background and sources to an article; developers and researchers share works in progress. Participants around the block or around the world can collaborate and converse, accessing one another's work through hyperlinked paths. Indeed, the Openlaw project—an online discussion of these very legal issues—has grown mainly through word-of-Web: participants discover Openlaw as they follow hyperlinks from other Web pages. The website that serves as one of the group's focal points consists in large part of a collection of hyperlinks drawing far-flung references together in a virtual archive.

## Argument
## I. Hyperlinks Are Core Elements of Expression on the Web

*2600* is a new publisher in a new medium, but it is entitled to the same First Amendment protection it needs to disseminate its news and commentary as are established publishers in traditional media. "[O]ur cases provide no basis for qualifying the level of First Amendment scrutiny that should be applied to this medium," the Supreme Court has held. *Reno v. ACLU*, 521 U.S. at 870. The Internet is a democratizing medium: "Through the use of Web pages … [any] individual can become a pamphleteer." *Id.* Hyperlinks are the paths among websites, creating the bustling street corners for distribution of those pamphlets and inviting passersby to engage more deeply with the issues raised. The Court should not permit plaintiffs to silence these crossroads.

In seeking to expand the injunction beyond direct distribution of the DeCSS utility to hyperlinking to other websites that legally offer it, plaintiffs go beyond the bounds of law and logic. HTML links are simply elements in a formal citation syntax, by which one website can refer to another much as a judicial opinion or legal brief refers to its precedents. A web page with hypertext links does not "provide" the content offered at the target pages merely by referencing those pages. Plaintiffs correctly do not seek to hold *2600* accountable for the content of linked-to pages, yet they attempt to cut the site out of the Web by denying it the ability to make references to those pages.

## A. A Hyperlink Is a Reference

Like most sites on the World Wide Web, *2600*'s web pages contain hyperlinks. Visitors to a website can click on words or pictures that are hyperlinked at that website and be taken to another location, often another website that is relevant to the hyperlinked word or picture. A hyperlink (of the form <a href=" Location">Label</a>) associates or "links" the Label with the target Location. The link syntax is part of HyperText Markup Language ("HTML"), which also allows Web authors to format text to add emphasis or design layout. *See, e.g.,* HTML 4.01 specification *<<http://www.w3.org/TR/html401/>>*. HTML is a set of computer instructions that enhance the expressive content of speech. In a hyperlink, Location is a reference to one of a number of other resources, most commonly another website—for which the prefix "http://" indicates that a user's browser can follow the link with HyperText Transfer Protocol. The Label, delimited by opening and closing "anchor" tags, may be text or an image, and is highlighted or underlined by most browsers. The href attribute in the opening tag ("<a ...>") gives the Location of the hypertext reference.[1] Hyperlinks are meta-text, giving weight or shading to speech as do the stage directions that accompany a play's script.

By comparison, a lawyer adds to a brief "*See* 483 L.Ed.2d 632." To those untrained in legal research, that (hypothetical) citation is nonsense. To those trained, however, it says "for further relevant information, go to page 632 of volume 483 of the second edition of the Lawyer's Edition version of the United States Supreme Court reports." The citation is both a reference and speech, even if of a particularized form understood only by those who understand legal citations. The layperson may have no idea what it means, but those who understand legal citations know it to say that there is further support for the brief's proposition at that location. Clearly, that reference serves as speech.

To a Web browser, however, one might say, "See <a href="*http://caselaw.findlaw.com/cgi-bin/getcase.pl?court=US&navby=case&vol=000&invol=98-1682* <*http://caselaw.findlaw.com/cgi-bin/getcase.pl?court=US&amp;navby=case&amp;vol=000&invol=98-1682*>">United States v. Playboy Enter-tainment Group</a>, in which the Supreme Court recently reaffirmed that content-based restrictions on speech must be justified by a compelling state interest and must be implemented by the least restrictive means possible." The hyperlink is a reference, but it is also speech, here saying that the proposition argued for is further supported by the linked site.

Much writing, legal and otherwise, is designed to persuade. Other things being equal, a hyperlink has more persuasive force and credibility than an unadorned URL or case name, since the ease of access increases the likelihood that the reader will go to the linked page and see for himself that the support exists. The legal citation and the hyperlink are both references and persuasive speech because they help to convince the reader that the speech has foundation.

By linking, the Web author often implicitly asserts that the target page is relevant to the discussion on his page. It may be a supporting element of foundation or background, an opposing viewpoint, a suggestion for further research, or simply an item of interest. The author may specifically disclaim endorsement of the content of the linked page, as the *New York Times*, <<*http://www.nytimes.com*>> does, but his link states that for those interested in his speech, the page to which he hyperlinks will also be of interest.

Thus, links contribute to the expressiveness of Web pages. Plaintiffs seem to think that simply by calling them "software," they can transform hyperlinks from expressive content into unprotected non-speech. (Proposed Order ¶ 1(e)) They err. "The fact that a medium of expression has a functional capacity should not preclude constitutional protection." *Junger v. Daley*, 209 F.3d 481. Indeed, to the extent that a hyperlink is functional, because it permits a reader more easily to move between Web pages, that "function" enhances the communication. Links allow Web authors to engage in dialogues, to add authority to their writings, and to create virtual associations of sites expressing similar opinions or disparate opinions on a unifying topic. As the Web's creator, physicist Tim Berners-Lee, describes it,

The dream behind the Web is of a common information space in which we communicate by sharing information. Its universality is essential: the fact that a hypertext link can point to anything, be it personal, local or global, be it draft or highly polished.[2]

To ban linking is to hamper all of these forms of First Amendment expression.

Plaintiffs repeat an argument that has been rejected now by two circuit courts of appeals: that a functional component can negate the protection of expression. This reasoning was flatly rejected in both *Bernstein v. U. S. Dept. of Justice*, 176 F.3d 1132, *withdrawn by* 192 F.3d 1308 (1999), and *Junger v. Daley*, 209 F.3d 481 (2000). Although the Ninth Circuit decision in *Bernstein* was withdrawn after the export policy at issue was revised, its analysis, endorsed by the Sixth Circuit in *Junger*, is sound:

[T]he government's argument, distilled to its essence, suggests that even one drop of "direct functionality" overwhelms any constitutional protections that expression might otherwise enjoy. This cannot be so. The distinction urged on us by the government would prove too much in this era of rapidly evolving computer capabilities. The fact that computers will soon be able to respond directly to spoken commands, for example, should not confer on the government the unfettered power to impose prior restraints on speech in an effort to control its "functional" aspects. The First Amendment is concerned with expression, and we reject the notion that the admixture of functionality necessarily puts expression beyond the protections of the Constitution. *Bernstein*, 176 F.3d at 1142.

Links are neither automatic nor infallible: Like legal or bibliographic citations, links are precise specifications of their targets. They are not necessarily accurate, however. Although a library patron retrieves a precise call number from the card catalog, he may not find the book on the shelf when he heads to the stacks; it may be checked out, misshelved, or on a table nearby. The case at the pin-cited page may not stand for what its proponent claims. Likewise, on the *2600* Web page, at least 74 of the links are currently "broken," such that no Web page is found at their target Locations. (Boyden Supplemental Decl.) Moreover, the Label's description of the content at the distant website may no longer—or never—match the page retrieved. The author of a Web page has no control over pages on other sites to which he links, and can only describe (or misdescribe) them at the time he edits the page.

A hyperlink's "function" is to help reduce the number of mouse or key clicks required to get from one web page to another with a web browser, making a user's pursuit of information as seamless as possible. If the website's location were specified in text rather than as a hyperlink, a cut and paste operation (of several clicks) of the address into the browser would still direct the browser to the remote page. Plaintiffs would have us believe that the Constitution permits chilling speech and threatening the heart of a global communications medium so long as an inferior method of speaking remains. This has never been part of First Amendment jurisprudence. Indeed, only last week, the Supreme Court reaffirmed that "special consideration or latitude is not accorded to the Government merely because the law can somehow be described as a burden rather than outright suppression." *United States v. Playboy Entertainment Group, Inc.,*—U.S. —, 2000 U.S. LEXIS 3427, No. 98-1682 (May 22, 2000).

## B. 2600 Is Using Hyperlinks for First Amendment Expression and Association

Plaintiffs take particular issue with a page from *2600*'s news archive describing plaintiffs' threats and inviting supporters to "mirror" the DeCSS files, to post them not for the technically implausible purpose of copying DVDs but to help maintain the free flow of information that is needed for continued investigation of the technology. The Web page, *<<http://www.2600.com/news/1999/1227-help.html>>*, is a protest akin to a union picket line or peaceful demonstration. Rather than take out a newspaper advertisement with the names of its supporters, *2600* publishes a page in its Web magazine linking to their websites. Beneath the page text, under the heading "Mirrors," is a list of websites in which each listed site is hyperlinked to its location on the Web. Thus as advertisers in the *New York Times* list their sponsors, *2600* gives the addresses at which its supporters can be contacted and their speech read. Site owners choose to express their political support not only by writing and hosting the linked web pages but by "signing" the magazine's list and making their pages publicly visible.

The plaintiffs contend that this constitutes "distribution" of DeCSS, and that it continues *2600*'s role as a "supplier" of DeCSS. Their assertions defy the common meanings of these words. Both of these claims fail because the *2600* website does not host or offer DeCSS. The *2600* website is as much a distributor of DeCSS as the Yellow Pages are distributors of pizza. *2600* is no more a supplier of DeCSS than the *New York Times* is a supplier of drugs when it reports that crack is being sold on a particular corner in Harlem or a court is by describing in an opinion materials it deems obscene and giving a volume and page number for the magazine where they are found.

The *2600* mirror list offers only information. No *2600* resources are used to transmit DeCSS. Once a user has retrieved the mirror list, he need have no further contact with *2600*, whether or not he chooses to follow a link from the page. If the user chooses to access the speech at one of the linked sites, his click on a link will be interpreted by the browser as a request directly to the remote site named in the "Location" tag. Assuming that site is online, it responds directly to the user with no assistance from *2600*. The mechanical aspect of the hyperlink in facilitating the transfer of information is inseparable from its expressive function in communicating the information.

Plaintiffs would bar *2600* from creating hyperlinks precisely for the communicative impact of those links: The multitude of links suggests that numerous people support *2600*'s fight for fair use of digital media; they express a shared view that reverse engineering justifies bypassing access controls; they imply that DeCSS is still easy to obtain and that an injunction against a single Web publisher will be ineffective to stem dissemination of DeCSS. It is not a message plaintiffs want to hear, but it is still not one they can block from the Web.

## II. Plaintiffs Seek a Content-Based Restriction of Speech

Plaintiffs disagree with the message of *2600* and its supporters that fair use must be preserved in digital media and that information formats should be widely accessible and interoperable. Because they dislike *2600*'s opinions, they seek to enlist this Court's aid in shutting down the lines of communication among these websites, among the individuals and groups behind them, and among citizens seeking to be informed on these issues. They seek a content-based restriction of speech that cannot withstand the strict scrutiny such regulations demand. Plaintiffs' proposed injunction would chill a broad range of protected speech because its enforcement depends on an individual examination of the content presented at the other end of every link.

Plaintiffs' attempts to bar *2600* from linking to outside sites would bar speech precisely for the message the links convey. The *2600* site explains its authors' motivations—and these are not piracy. As numerous declarants for defendants have shown, DeCSS is simply not a rational method for copying DVDs. As *2600* states, however, DeCSS must be kept available to preserve access to the programming ideas it contains. These ideas, fairly reverse engineered, have already contributed to the ongoing effort to provide a free and open source DVD player. Yet plaintiffs would have this Court assist them in blocking competition in the manufacture of DVD players. Plaintiffs seek novel assistance in reimplementing the "block booking" practices the Supreme Court has previously rejected. *See United States v. Paramount Pictures, Inc.*, 334 U.S. 131, 68 S.Ct. 915 (1948).

The communicative effect of the speech in *2600*'s hyperlinks—and the chilling effect that an injunction on hyperlinking would have—is not merely hypothetical. The logs of one linked site show 343 "hits" referred directly from the *2600* page. (See Smith Decl. Exh. B, referer log from the website <http://sam.rh.uchicago.edu/dvd/>) Three hundred forty-three people have followed the channel of communication from *2600* to this "Banned Software Archive"—343 readers have read ideas and political expression on this third-party site that they would be unable to reach so easily if *2600* were barred from linking to it. There is no reason to believe this site is unique among sites on the *2600* mirror list. Rather, its logs suggest that thousands of people overall would be deterred from finding the mirror sites' political expression if they could not get there from the listing on the *2600* site. Plaintiffs' suggestion that there is no harm because the hitherto-linked sites "will still exist" ignores the burden to speech of hiding the sites from public view. Even a burden, as opposed to an absolute bar on protected speech, faces strict scrutiny.

Content-based restrictions on speech demand the highest level of scrutiny. If laws must be struck down when they outlaw advocacy of the "duty, necessity, or propriety of violence" (*Brandenburg v. Ohio*, 395 U.S. 444, 447, 89 S.Ct. 1827 (1969)) or the burning of the American flag (*Texas v. Johnson*, 491 U.S. 397, 109 S.Ct. 2533 (1989)), mere reference to a computer program alleged to circumvent copyright or access controls clearly may not be enjoined. The First Amendment does not countenance such a prior restraint.

Barring hyperlinking to sites that contain, among other speech, code that itself has not yet had the benefit of a trial to determine its protected status would impose an extraordinary prior restraint on speech. Indeed, in § 1203(b)(1), Congress specifically warned that DMCA violations would not justify prior restraints. Against that explicit legislative caution, the Court should not enjoin linking or posting before the protected status of the underlying code has been adjudicated. *See* Mark Lemley & Eugene Volokh, *Freedom of Speech and Injunctions in Intellectual Property Cases*, 48 Duke L.J. 147 (1988).

# III. Plaintiffs Cannot Demonstrate a Contributory Violation of the DMCA

Finally, plaintiffs' claim that linking constitutes a contributory violation of the DMCA is too far outside the pale to be recognized. While we do not dispute that courts have found contributory liability for copyright infringement, no copyright infringement is even alleged in this case. Section 1201's prohibition on the distribution of circumvention devices, by contrast, is already a step removed from infringement or even "unauthorized access" to copyrighted works. Since circumvention devices are not inherently harmful, the anti-distribution provisions of § 1201(a)(2) and (b)(2) must be derived from liability for the potential copyright or paracopyright violations of those to whom devices are distributed. We join defendants' argument that these prohibitions already overstep First Amendment limits if they enjoin code—expressive speech. *See Junger v. Daley*, 209 F.3d 481. Taking yet another step back from the potential violations

by holding *2600* contributorily liable for possibly facilitating distribution of a device that hypothetically aids infringement and if so
could then potentially be used for copyright violations not only cuts
a huge swath of protected speech but stretches intent and foreseeability beyond recognition.

Section 1201(a)(1) prohibits the circumvention of technological
access control measures. When that provision takes effect, subject to
the exemptions issued by the Librarian of Congress in the current
rulemaking, individuals who use circumvention devices for unauthorized access to copyrighted works will be directly liable for their
activities. In addition, contrary to plaintiffs' assertion, Section 1201
does "expressly address contributory liability principles": 1201(a)(2)
imposes liability on those who "manufacture, import, offer to the
public, provide, or otherwise traffic in" access-control circumvention
devices because those contribute to the violations of their users. That
provision has built into it the *Sony* rule exempting devices with substantial non-infringing uses. Where the statute clearly delimits contributory liability, the Court must not craft additional layers further
removed from the primary violation of access-control circumvention. If the Court nonetheless finds the protected status of linking
unclear, it must weigh the speech and creative interests as the *Sony*
court did:

In a case like this, in which Congress has not plainly marked our
course, we must be circumspect in construing the scope of rights
created by a legislative enactment which never contemplated such
a calculus of interests. In doing so, we are guided by Justice
Stewart's exposition of the correct approach to ambiguities in the
law of copyright:

"The limited scope of the copyright holder's statutory monopoly,
like the limited copyright duration required by the Constitution,

reflects a balance of competing claims upon the public interest: Creative work is to be encouraged and rewarded, but private motivation must ultimately serve the cause of promoting broad public availability of literature, music, and the other arts...."

*Sony Corp. v. Universal City Studios*, 464 U.S. 417, 431-32, 104 S.Ct. 774 (1984) (citing *Twentieth Century Music Corp. v. Aiken*, 422 U.S. 151, 156, 95 S.Ct. 2040, 2043).

Even were "contributory violation of Section 1201(a)(2)" plausible in the abstract, plaintiffs cannot logically distinguish *2600*'s Web pages and hyperlinks from protected advocacy. Speech strongly urging a violation of the law is still protected speech, and plaintiffs cannot assert that displaying a link to DeCSS constitutes a "clear and present danger." *See Brandenburg v. Ohio*, 395 U.S. at 447. Moreover, plaintiffs' claim that links contribute to infringement fails the *Sony* test, which finds contributory liability only where the alleged contributor has no "substantial noninfringing uses." *Sony*, 464 U.S. at 441. *2600*'s links lead to pages that make political statements in text and code, whether or not their visitors download DeCSS. As that speech and the statement made by each page's presence do not violate the DMCA, giving access to those is a "substantial noninfringing use[]" of *2600*'s links.

# IV. DeCSS Fits Within the Reverse Engineering Exception of Section 1201(f), Either to Interoperate With Programs on DVDs or to Enable Interoperability of These Programs and Players on Unsupported Operating Systems

Plaintiffs incorrectly focus on the "functional" aspects of HTML in seeking to enlarge the injunction. Yet they ignore "functional" elements of the DVDs they seek to shield from reverse engineering. Their error is twofold, for the First Amendment protects even "functional" speech of facts and instructions, while the Copyright Act's protections are limited to expressive non-functional elements. Instead, the functional elements of a DVD justify the use of DeCSS as an implement of interoperability.

By the standard of functionality by which plaintiffs refer to the HTML on *2600*'s website as a set of software instructions, DVDs are clearly programs as defined in Title 17: "a set of statements or instructions to be used directly or indirectly in a computer in order to bring about a certain result." § 17 U.S.C. 101

While it appears to have been assumed that a DVD contains no software instructions at all, several functional elements are required on a DVD to allow the digital playing of a movie using today's technology. These include the commands that mark the movie to enable navigation through it; the commands used to store the video in a 'compressed' format; and the disk and title keys which are actually part of the fully constituted player program that descrambles a given movie.*[3]*

The defense brief correctly justifies the distribution of DeCSS as a tool for fostering interoperability between computer programs. Interoperability, as defined in § 1201(f), refers to exchange of information between at least two programs, one of which must be independently created software. DeCSS was created, in the words of Jon Johansen, "to add DVD support to Linux-and, of course, to other operating systems, such as FreeBSD."*[4]* DeCSS was adopted by a Linux reverse engineering project, LiViD (Linux Video and DVD), for the purpose of reverse engineering the DVD format in order to create an open source Linux DVD player. DeCSS was not created by the LiViD group, but by third parties who then made it available for a wide range of open source projects. DeCSS allowed independently created, open source DVD players to exchange information with operating systems that did not previously support DVD technology. It is a matter of record that DeCSS is useful in this regard. (See DiBona Decl.) DeCSS has also fostered interoperability between these independently created software DVD players and the software tools that are used to make or author DVDs.

DeCSS fosters program- and platform-independent use of information created and formatted by programs-this use is directly supported in the text of § 1201(f)(3):

[T]he means permitted under paragraph (2), may be made available to others if the person... provides such ... means solely for the purpose of enabling interoperability of an independently created computer program with other programs, and to the extent that doing so does not constitute infringement under this title or violate applicable law other than this section.

Paragraph (2) provides

Notwithstanding the provisions of subsections (a)(2) and (b), a person may develop and employ technological means to circumvent a technological measure, or to circumvent protection afforded by a technological measure,...for the purpose of enabling interoperability of an independently created computer program with other programs, if such means are necessary to achieve such interoperability, to the extent that doing so does not constitute infringement under this title.

The parts of this paragraph are disjunctive: The first part (before the "or") refers back to § 1201(f)(1), which speaks of circumventing a measure that "controls access to a particular portion of that program." This is the origin of the "programs only" argument. The second half of § 1201(f)(2), on the other hand, allows for much more than circumvention of access control to programs only.

Thus both § 1201(f)(2) and § 1201(f)(3) refer to interoperability with 'other' programs. A data format, which formats information shared between two programs, may be reverse engineered as well. The restriction here is that this is allowed only if it "does not constitute infringement". A purchased DVD is a mixture of programs and encrypted data formats. The formats have been reverse engineered to enable the licensed data contained therein to be passed between programs, allowing a purchaser to play the program he licensed by his purchase on the operating system of his choice. The distribution of DeCSS fits well under the law, when the legislative history is taken into account. In reading the legislative history, it is important not to take statements out of context. The "programs only" intent is accurate in the context of § 1201(f)(1), but cannot square with the intent of § 1201(f)(2) and § 1201(f)(3). The House of Representatives report puts special emphasis on "small software developers" where it discusses what became § 1201(f)(3). Open source software projects depend on the volunteer efforts of unpaid programmers who devote their time to giving to the commons. This is the archetype of a "small software developer" that makes § 1201(f)(3) most applicable.

Similarly, § 1201(f)(3) recognizes that developing complex computer programs often involves the efforts of many persons. For example, some of these persons may be hired to develop a specific portion of the final product. For that person to perform these tasks, some of the information acquired through the permitted analysis, and the tools to accomplish it, may have to be made available to that person. The subsection allows developers of independently created software to rely on third parties either to develop the necessary circumvention tools, or to identify the necessary information to achieve interoperability. The ability to rely on third parties is particularly important for small software developers who do not have the capability of performing these functions in-house. This provision permits such sharing of information and tools.

Section 1201(f)(3) applies where, as here, reverse engineering does not otherwise constitute infringement. DVDs are published media to which fair use rights apply. Creation of technological circumvention measures which are useable only on purchased media are not in themselves infringing, due to fair use rights of the public. Reverse engineering of such media is fair use, and distribution of the tools used in such fair use is sanctioned under § 1201(f)(3).

# *Conclusion*

For the foregoing reasons, plaintiffs' motion to modify the preliminary injunction should be denied and the preliminary injunction should be vacated.
Dated: May 30, 2000
Respectfully submitted,

---

Margaret E. Smith
THE BERKMAN CENTER FOR INTERNET & SOCIETY
AT HARVARD LAW SCHOOL
1563 Massachusetts Avenue,
Cambridge, Massachusetts 02138
(617) 495-7547
....

---

...

*[1]* Berners-Lee et al., Uniform Resource Identifiers (URI): Generic Syntax: RFC 2396, <<*http://www.ietf.org/rfc/rfc2396.txt>>*; Uniform Resource Locators (URL): RFC 1738, <<*http://www.ietf.org/rfc/rfc1738.txt>>*.

*[2]* Tim Berners-Lee, *The World Wide Web: A very short personal history*, <*http://www.w3.org/People/Berners-Lee/ShortHistory.html* <*http://www.linuxworld.com/linuxworld/lw-2000-01/f_lw-01-dvd-interview.html>>*.

*[3]* First, a DVD contains instructions in a computer file that accompanies the video. These instruction are typically used to create 'chapter' headings and, much like hyperlinks, to allow the DVD viewer to jump to specific points in the movie instantly.

Second, the audio and video pictures are 'compressed' using a format called MPEG2. MPEG2 video is an ISO/IEC standard that specifies the syntax and semantics of an encoded video bitstream. These include parameters such as bit rates, picture sizes and resolutions that may be applied, and how it is decoded to reconstruct the picture.

Finally, to decode a DVD requires three different kinds of keys: player, disk, and title keys. The disk and title keys are found on the DVD itself, and are thus licensed when the DVD is purchased. These keys are part of the program that decrypts CSS, and are legitimate targets for reverse engineering under § 1201(f)(1).

*[4]* J.S. Kelly, "Meet the Kid Behind the DVD Hack," LinuxWorld Magazine interview with Jon Johansen, January 31, 2000. <<*http://www.linuxworld.com/linuxworld/lw-2000-01/f_lw-01-dvd-interview.html>>*

*note: Other Amici were submitted by members of the press and other organizations.*
*LINK =*

# Appendix V
## President Clinton's Statement to DMCA

http://www.pub.whitehouse.gov/uri-res/I2R?urn:pdi://oma.eop.gov.us/1998/10/29/16.text.1

THE WHITE HOUSE

Office of the Press Secretary

---

For Immediate Release                    October 28, 1998

### STATEMENT BY THE PRESIDENT

Today I am pleased to sign into law H.R. 2281, the "Digital Millennium Copyright Act." This Act implements two landmark treaties that were successfully negotiated by my Administration in 1996 and to which the Senate gave its advice and consent to ratification on October 21, 1998. The Act also limits the liability of online service providers for copyright infringement under certain conditions.

The World Intellectual Property Organization (WIPO) Copyright Treaty and the WIPO Performances and Phonogram Treaty mark the most extensive revision of international copyright law in over 25 years. The treaties will grant writers, artists, and other creators of copyrighted material global protection from piracy in the digital age.

245

These treaties will become effective at a time when technological innovations present us with great opportunities for the global distribution of copyrighted works. These same technologies, however, make it possible to pirate copyrighted works on a global scale with a single keystroke. The WIPO treaties set clear and firm standards— obligating signatory countries to provide "adequate legal protection" and "effective legal remedies" against circumvention of certain technologies that copyright owners use to protect their works, and against violation of the integrity of copyright management information. This Act implements those standards, carefully balancing the interests of both copyright owners and users.

I am advised by the Department of Justice that certain provisions of H.R. 2281 and the accompanying Conference Report regarding the Register of Copyrights raise serious constitutional concerns. Contrary to assertions in the Conference Report, the Copyright Office is, for constitutional purposes, an executive branch entity. Accordingly, the Congress may exercise its constitutionally legitimate oversight powers to require the Copyright Office to provide information relevant to the legislative process. However, to direct that Office's operations, the Congress must act in accord with the requirements of bicameralism and presentment prescribed in Article I of the Constitution. Further, the Congress may not require the Register to act in a manner that would impinge upon or undermine the President's discretion under Article II, section 3 of the Constitution to determine which, if any, executive branch recommendations to the Congress would be "necessary and expedient." Accordingly, I will construe sections 103(a), 104(b), 401(b), and 403(a) of H.R. 2281 to require the Register to perform duties only insofar as such requirements are consistent with these constitutional principles.

From the efforts of the Assistant Secretary of Commerce and Commissioner of Patents and Trademarks who acted as the lead negotiator for these treaties, to the agreement reached by interests affected by online service provider liability, to the improvements added by two House Committees and one Senate Committee, this Act reflects the diligence and talents of a great many people. Through enactment of the Digital Millennium Copyright Act, we have done our best to protect from digital piracy the copyright industries that comprise the leading export of the United States.

WILLIAM J. CLINTON

THE WHITE HOUSE,
October 28, 1998.

30-30-30

-----

## TO THE POLITICIANS/Lawmakers

## ONE FINAL QUESTION:
### Where are the answers?

www.ingramcontent.com/pod-product-compliance
Lightning Source LLC
Chambersburg PA
CBHW021141070326
40689CB00043B/841

* 9 7 8 0 5 9 5 1 6 0 0 4 4 *